PARENTING A BUSINESS

IF YOU CAN RAISE A CHILD, YOU CAN RUN A BUSINESS

BY

JEREMY CORTEZ

I0073869

Copyright © 2018 by Jeremy Cortez

All rights reserved. No part of this publication may be reproduced, distributed, or transmitted in any form or by any means, including photocopying, recording, or other electronic or mechanical methods, without the prior written permission of the publisher, except in the case of brief quotations embodied in critical reviews and certain other noncommercial uses permitted by copyright law. For permission requests, write to the publisher at the address below.

Tyler@authorsunite.com

Published by AuthorsUnite.com

Acknowledgements

First and foremost, I have to thank my amazing wife, Veronica. Whether it'd be our late night talks about the book content to taking care of our boys while I wrote, this book would not be possible without you. I am grateful to have your continuous love and support. Thank you, my love.

Thank you to my two sons, Sebastian and Elliott, for giving me the education I needed to become a successful business owner. Your simple teachings of life have given me the focus and energy I needed to make all my dreams come true. Not bad for being under the age of 2!

To my parents, Josie and Cesar, thank you for raising me and giving me every opportunity to succeed. With your guidance, I learned vital lessons of entrepreneurship that are covered throughout this book, such as hard work, sacrifice, focus, persistence, and resilience.

A special thanks to Kim O'Hara, my intuitive book coach at A Story Inside. Thank you for all the supportive texts and calls every week I freaked out writing this book, for the accountability to keep writing despite all the excuses I could come up with, and for all the guidance on making me a better writer and author.

Thank you to Tyler Wagner and the whole publishing team, Authors Unite. I realized that after experiencing the accomplishment of writing my first book, the job had just BEGUN... I truly appreciate everything you've done for the success of this book, from the book cover design to all your marketing and business strategies.

Finally, a special shout out to my friends and family, and fellow business owners and parents. You've all helped me along my journey as a business owner, parent, and author. Thank you for sharing all your perspectives about the parenting of a business, and showing me how much value I have to give to the world. Without your perspectives, I would have not been able to shift forward in the manifestation of this book. I would be less than without the continued support and love from: Jill Jacob, Rachel Brooks, Nestor Perez, Jessica Mah, Peggy Neidig, Stella Yu, Derek Wong, Teresa Reif, Julie Castenada, Rose Gutierrez, Chris Cortez, Aurora Cortez, Elena Licari, Heather Delaney, Julie Manubay, Jenna Davi, and Brenda Simson.

And to all the parents I have not yet met that are out there dreaming of their businesses.... I did this. So can you.

Table of Contents

Introduction

What brings me the most joy in life are *breakthroughs*. When our perceptions shift and our minds expand, we learn, attempt, succeed and grow. These actions are all parts of the sum that creates a breakthrough for a business owner, as well as a parent. So I connected the dots, and my breakthrough directed me to create another business... for me, and for YOU. I love breakthroughs because they have the power to change your entire perspective and alter your destiny. Being able to be part of THAT gets me out of bed every morning.

I've been blessed to witness many shifts in perceptions with people I connect with, whether they are current clients or people I meet in passing. I could be at a kid's birthday party, a meditation group, a conference in New Orleans, or a family dinner. At any given moment, I meet people, listen to their stories, and provide whatever insights I can to help them move forward with their desires. As a result, their perspectives shift. I get to see the glimmer of hope in their eyes and excitement they have throughout their whole demeanor... and I am hooked. My passion in life is to help others have their own breakthroughs for success, and identify what that means to them.

I am a seeker. Always have been. It drives my wife nuts sometimes. I chomp on the bit. I can effortlessly see visions of greatness in others, which fuels my excitement to see them succeed. Because of this ability, I am called to be the guinea pig, experiencing breakthroughs in my thinking, to help others experience their own breakthroughs. I've read books, attended seminars, interviewed and connected with people across the world, challenging my current beliefs and adjusting my "truth" with fluidity. I have even had a few days of just staring at the computer screen going, "Hmmm, what's next?"

In my journey to help people reach their own breakthroughs in life, my "job" is to put myself out there and connect with people. I've attended countless seminars, joined business and networking groups, local training communities and parenting circles. When I joined the latter group, I saw many parents venting their frustrations about their job situations. They would say, "I want to do something else with my life, I just don't know what that is or where to start." Or "I'm a stay-at-home parent looking to start my own business, but I'm not qualified to begin." Then, they'd see me building multiple businesses and parenting two young boys, wondering how I was able to make that happen.

I'd find myself being interviewed by these parents, asking about how I got started, how I managed so much, and how I was able to stay "fulfilled" through it all. Then these same parents expressed their fears of starting their own business. They were afraid of losing time with their family, or felt like building a business is too risky. Others felt their dreams of entrepreneurship were too big, or they needed to have capital first. My heart sank every time I hear them trapped in their perspectives. I knew I had to take action and help them in some way.

I decided to dig deeper with them, asking about their fears, doubts, and frustrations they thought were unfounded or not related to having business success. It is all related! I was filled with excitement. I saw their breakthroughs were just a perspective shift away from changing their whole lives. I jumped on the opportunity to help them change their lives.

Being a father of two boys and a serial entrepreneur, I possessed a profound truth that has given me the success I've always wanted, ever since I was old enough to define what success meant to me. This breakthrough has been so transformational in my life that I knew I had to share it with these parents, and the rest of the world. I stepped outside my comfort zone and took an action I've never done before, nor ever dreamed about doing in the past... I wrote this book.

Parenting A Business is a book that parallels the similarities between parenting and business, showing how your life experience as a parent has provided you a significant edge to be successful in business adventures. My goal is to simplify the concept of business for you in a way that is easy to understand, especially in how it relates to the day in and day out of being a parent. I will demonstrate that your parenting experiences have groomed you to run your own company, even if you're not aware. You will be provided a shift that many parents have experienced with me one on one. With that shift, you will have the opportunity to venture off in the entrepreneurial space and see what you're made of.

I'll tell you real life stories about other parents who've shared their fears and doubts, along with their hopes and dreams of starting a business. I'll share suggestions and provide a guide of how to get started in a business, comparing the preparation to having your first child. Most importantly, I will provide you a roadmap of how to create a business, from beginning to end, demystifying the complexities of a business into very easy action steps.

And here is a caveat... I don't believe everyone should run their own business. So this book, if you do the steps within, will show you without wasting lots of time and money, if you have what it takes to be a business owner. By the time you've finished the book, you will have some kind of breakthrough - I assure you of that - but it will be personal to who you want to be and what you've been looking for.

Thank you for giving me the opportunity to guide you on this path. I look forward to hearing *your* stories. I still have a lot to learn.

Stay inspired,

J.C.

Chapter 1

My Best Year in Business ... Ever

"You are far more prepared than you think."

I was sitting in the balcony of my hotel suite, overlooking a breathtaking San Diego sunset, when I realized I'd achieved every single goal mapped out for my photography business since I started the company in 2011. "Impossible" yearly revenue goals had been met. I'd worked with a Fortune 500 company. I'd been published in numerous magazines and ad promotions. And here's the best part: I had accomplished it all while working, on average, less than 30 hours a week.

As I shared my success with friends and family, I was asked a series of questions: "How did you do it?" "What books did you read?" "What was your breakthrough point?" "What helped give you the edge to achieve the success in a seemingly oversaturated marketplace?" Everyone wanted to know my secret.

There is no secret. But as I answered their questions as honestly as I could, I heard in my head the real reason for my success.

I had started a whole bunch of businesses over the years. Most had failed. But this was the first time I was in business *and* a parent. That was the winning equation.

My photography business altered its destiny the *moment* I became a parent in 2015. With the birth of my son Seba came the unexpected, unplanned-for evolution of my approach as a business owner.

Before he was born, a good friend (and successful entrepreneur) had predicated, "Your son will make you a better business owner." At the time he told me this, I'd no idea what he meant or what he saw. I just hoped he was right.

In a sense, my business career started when I was in grade school. I helped my family with multi-level marketing companies from nutrition to personal safety alarms. I would wear the personal safety alarms to school, encouraging my classmates to tell their parents, and demonstrate how they worked in class. Other times, I would talk to parents and ask them about their nutrition goals and how the protein shake products could help them. And yes, I attempted to sell these products when I was eight years old.

My mom always had the entrepreneurial spirit and constantly encouraged me to help with her business ventures. When I was 16 years old, she created a business certifying care homes for the elderly and convinced me to get certified too so I could help grow the business.

By the time I was 19, I was introduced to Tony Robbins and wanted to follow in his footsteps. I took courses and was certified to be a life coach. It fell through not because the clients would push back on my qualifications, but because I bought into not having the resources I needed.

Various multi-level marketing business models followed, ranging from telecommunications, travel, and juice companies, all of which were started and abandoned. With a track record of marginal success, I couldn't help but see how right my friend had been: The factor that had changed everything for me, business-wise, was my new role as a father. Most parents worry that their children will slow down their businesses. For me, it was the contrary. My son's entry into my life had blessed me with good fortune.

Or was there more to these results?

My Fear

When Sebastian was born, my photography business was undergoing a repeat of all my past failed businesses. I wasn't making much money, I had marginal marketing in place, and I constantly worried where the next project would turn up. I had narrowed my niche to business and marketing photography. Occasionally, I would help out in other categories, but the company barely made ends meet and I was concerned I would have to get a "real job."

To make matters more complicated, my wife and I had decided we were not going to put Seba in daycare his first year. We had worked out a schedule where we'd split the workweek to watch him and use our off-days to work. I agreed to take 2 extra weekdays off to watch him.

Agreeing to this new schedule put a lot of stress on me. Staying home seemed like the right decision as we would save money on daycare, but I was terrified that my photography business would suffer. Most of my photography projects were conducted on weekdays, so cutting the availability in half sounded like business suicide. After making that decision, the thought of getting a regular job seemed rather attractive. It could provide security and stability for my family.

My wife planned on going back to work three months after Seba was born. I had till then to get organized and figure out a system for managing family life with business life. I hired an assistant to take care of all the inbound leads, booking processes, and social media updates. I was also very mindful about how much energy I would need to devote to both jobs: being a parent and running my business. Limiting the number of days I was available forced me to cluster all my photo projects into isolated time frames.

Soon some of my dad days started as just that: Diaper change—CHECK, morning 4-ounce bottle of milk—CHECK, change of clothes—CHECK, our morning dance routine (since neither of us drank coffee)—CHECK. Sebastian and I would make our way to the kitchen to hang out. He would sit on his "command center" (the infant jumper seat with toys surrounding the seat) playing and drooling all over his activities while I would work on the business. On my remaining days, I'd be out photographing clients.

After four months on this schedule, I began calculating the financials of my business for the previous months. I suspected the numbers wouldn't be too great as I'd just started to come back and build some momentum. I braced myself for some harsh results and steeled myself for some disheartening numbers. Once all the numbers had been tallied, though, I stared at them in disbelief.

I had made more money in the previous month than in any month since I started the business ... and that was *after* I had slashed two "work days" off my schedule. Not knowing what had happened, I redid the numbers. Surely, I made an error in my calculations. But the same number magically appeared. "Okay," I told myself, "human error. Try one more time." Same numbers.

How could this be? What was so different about what I did in the previous months and years from what I did that month—other than limiting my availability by two weekdays? What was so different in my routine that I could actualize such results? Asking those questions gave me some great insights.

In that moment, I knew my friend was right. Parenting limited the amount of "extra time" I had, forcing me to prioritize my actions and get clear on what mattered most—both professionally and personally. I evolved into a better business owner, seeing compounding success with my new approach.

The arrival of this beautiful child who destroys diapers with pure will, who cries and screams every four hours, who tests the limits of my sanity, turned me into a savvy business owner capable of reaching his goals. His presence was the reason I achieved everything I wanted in such a surprising fashion.

I had no plan to inspire parents or teach what I've learned about reaching success as a parent. I was creating goals for the coming year, the "next steps" with the photography business. For instance, if my goal was to make one dollar, the next year I would set a goal to make two dollars.

Yet as I did the planning, all the goals for my business became uninspiring. And I saw that this "next level" for my business wasn't something that interested me. I found that after reaching this benchmark in my photography business, I was hungry for something deeper: A new venture about parenting and creating a business.

This new business notion scared the crap out of me. For a good portion of my business life, I had a vision of what I wanted from my photography business but never planned for what happens once I conquered that mountain. I tried other types of photography, did some creative work, tried to go back and photograph what used to inspire me. But after all that effort, I still found myself empty and unfulfilled. It was a very important crossroads in my life. I realized this business had run its course for me.

I started searching all over again, trying to find what the "next chapter" held for me. My searching met with very little success. The photography business was thriving even with me putting little effort into it, thus, giving me the benefit of time to search and reflect.

Why would I even consider starting a new business? Months went by with no answers. I searched everywhere for clues as to what I should do next. I attended more seminars, read more books, participated in more networking events. I even asked my two-year-old for advice. I'm confident he gave me the correct advice, but I wasn't educated enough to decipher what he was saying. Finally, I reached out to a member of my mastermind group, an extremely successful entrepreneur whose insight and business savvy I trusted.

We talked about some principles when looking for new ventures and strategies on how to qualify them. I was focusing on results, goals, and visions to aspire to, while she was getting me to focus elsewhere.

She said something to me I'll never forget: "Jeremy, the life I'm living isn't one I chose; it chose me. I didn't consciously choose to be a business owner. Look at your life right now. Look at what is calling you now, no matter how odd it feels."

Then I saw it was right in front of me: Helping parents become better business owners. In fact, I wanted to run with the idea that parents are much more "qualified" to run their own businesses than many people! They are highly qualified, and I wanted to help them.

Then I ran into my first challenge: Do parents WANT to be business owners? Do they even care that they are qualified? No sooner had I asked those questions that the answers came to me in the memories of friends—also parents—telling me how they wished they could run their own businesses. They'd sigh about how "lucky" I was to be able to create a business doing something I loved to do. I'd hear their brilliant business ideas and could see how successful they would be if they followed through. But then they'd share all their fears and anxieties of not being qualified or ready to start a business. These recollections prompted me to pursue my idea of helping parents further.

A large part of my parenting experiences mirrored my business experiences. As I looked back at every business I'd created, every business seminar and networking event I'd attended, and every book I'd read, all related the same range of theories about business—but being a parent gave you the "real life" experiences that parallel that of running a business.

Have you ever listened to successful entrepreneurs who tell you how the companies they created are like their children? This is no coincidence. Before having my son, I treated my business like it was my own child. I gave it all the attention it needed, nurtured it, cared for it, and helped it in any way to grow.

Can you recall being a first-time parent? Did you read every book, go to every class, and read every blog about being a parent? You created a plan, baby-proofed your home, and were ready to BE A PARENT. Remember all that? Then what happened?

Your child came into this world and all that education flew right out the window along with your sleep and sanity. At that moment, you just got accepted to the school of hard knocks and the fail-forward academy. You learned how to be a parent by actually being a parent. No book, seminar, or video could've given you the experiences that would turn you into a parent. You *experienced* what it was like to run on no sleep. You *experienced* what it was like to change a blowout diaper for the first time in a public place. You *experienced* all the frustrations of an inconsolable child who cries through the night—and you learned how to handle it. You *experienced* a child who cries when his mom is at work, making the hours of the day feel like years! You *experienced* a child who'd eaten his meal only to throw it all up— all over you? And sometimes you experienced all of the above in one day ... and how much more would you experience until he moves out and goes to college?!

What if I were to tell you that a majority of these events are very similar to that of running a business? What if I were to tell you that behind all the SEO strategies, the accounts payable, the contracts, the marketing, the sales, the product development, the hiring ... were basic strategies you've already conquered as a parent? How would you feel if you knew you were already groomed to run a business?

So, if there is something inside you that yearns to create your own business, you are far more prepared than you think.

I tested my theory with a friend of mine. I was helping her with some strategies on her business model and how to scale. She felt dismayed that she'd never taken business classes in school. Without hesitation, my subconscious took over and said out loud, "You're a parent of two. You are much more qualified than you think."

She had no idea what I was talking about. I assured her that she had it within her to make this business successful. I spent some time laying out the very tools that I will share with you in this book.

I would dare to state that the average parent is more qualified to start a business than the average business graduate. The life experience, the self-awareness when crisis hits, the understanding of yourself, and your capabilities far exceed academic theory learned from a book. You've developed the emotional muscles that support you in times of crisis and conflict. Over the years of mastering your parenting skills, you've unknowingly developed habits and strategies that work just as well in business as they do with your kids.

If you're reading this book, my guess is that you are a parent, and you have an itch to become an entrepreneur. There might be a business idea that you've been thinking about in the back (or the front) of your mind but haven't done anything about. You might be waiting for the perfect situation, the perfect timing, or the perfect partner to start. You might be making plans in your head but haven't put them to paper, reading all the recommended books about business building but haven't applied any of it, or just preparing for the day you *decide* to take action. The majority of these inactions are based on some level of fear, doubt, or stress you associate with starting a business.

Here are the most common fears I have encountered (and personally subjected myself to in the past). By the end of this book, you'll have the tools to boldly answer these fears yourself.

Jeremy's Common Fears

- *As a parent, where will I find the time or energy to run a business?*

- *I don't know how to start a business. Where do I begin?*

- *My idea will never work.*

- *I don't have the resources (i.e., investment capital, connections/contacts)*

- *I don't have the education.*

- *I don't have the personality to own a business.*

- *I don't have the time to start a business.*

- *What if it fails?*

- *What if it succeeds and time with my kid(s) suffers?*

- *What if no one likes my idea? What if no one buys it?*

Once we are willing to be honest about our fears and insecurities, we give ourselves permission to explore the courage to take action.

Get honest about what you desire in your life. If you're honest enough, you can stare down the fear and never let it control you ever again.

But first consider these questions:

- Are you the stay-at-home parent who is considering making a little extra money on the side? *Keep reading.*

- Are you a parent of older kids, and are you curious about starting a new business, but don't know if you can or where to start? *Keep reading.*

- Are you in a career that doesn't utilize all of your talents, but know you can't leave your 9-5 job because of all the responsibilities you have to your family? *Keep reading.*

- You wanted to start your own business but didn't know what kind of business or how to find it? *Keep reading.*

Still reading? Clearly, you are intrigued.

Being a parent is one of life's hardest jobs. We are responsible for another human life. We alter our own lives in service of another that's solely dependent on us. No amount of education or life experience can prepare us for being a first-time parent. We plunge into that role and do the best that we can. So, if you are a parent, you have my utmost respect and honor. My desire is for you to be able to explore other adventures that life has to offer. Like parenting, business may not be easy, but it's be worth it.

Shall we begin?

Chapter 2

Why You? Why Now?

"Get curious!"

I am well-aware that not everyone should own their own business. The days can be long, the road can be tough, and it's not for the faint of heart. My commitment is to guide you to discovering whether your desire to create a business is an itch you should further scratch.

Within these pages I will present relatable scenarios to show you that you can be resourceful and capable enough to run your own company.

First, a Question:

To start this journey, there is a key question you'll need to ask yourself. Your answer will assist you in laying the foundation for creating your business. Answering this question will help you get to the root about what's really motivating you toward starting a business. Answering it will help determine whether you *should* be in business or not. That question is (drum roll please):

Why are you now curious about starting a business now?

In the time I've started and stopped over ten entrepreneurial enterprises, here are the top reasons why people I knew contemplated starting a business. As you review this list, please remember that being a parent is a leg up to starting a business, not a detriment. Here's the list:

- *You're surrounded by stories of people who've found success in business and want to try it out for yourself.*

- *You're a top employee within a company and find that your ideas for how to better the company and provide more value to customers are constantly rejected. So, you've decided that you can do better on your own.*

- *You've done side projects such as event planning, preparing/styling food, handiwork, teaching, writing, or motivating, and constantly hear from people that you need to start your own business.*

- *You're at an unfulfilling job and want a change. You know there's more to life than working a job that doesn't fulfill you, but don't know what that is.*

- *You have always wanted to run your own business, but feel you don't have the education or qualifications to run it.*

- *You're tired of living the life that others have created for you.*

- *You want to start a business, but don't have a particular skillset that you think can make a business.*

- *You see a NEED that isn't being met in the world, and you deeply desire to fulfill that need.*

If one of the above reasons resonates with you, the message is simple: You know why you are curious. As you'll see later in this chapter, knowing the reason WHY you're curious is all you need at this moment to consider starting a business.

Your Circumstances

Determining why you want to start is just the beginning. You also need to understand the scope of where you currently are when you start. The circumstances of your life have influenced your action—or lack thereof.

You must allow yourself to understand why you haven't taken action in the past, so you can address that mindset or situation and take different action in the future. In the world of parenting, there are countless situations and circumstances that make our experiences unique. It's the same with starting and running a business.

There are three types of parent categories. Each offers a lot of excuses to not start a business, but at the same time, offers the greatest reasons to start one. I have personal experience with all three categories.

The W-2 Parent

Are you a parent who has the "traditional" 9-5 job, working five days a week? You work for a company, report to a manager of some sort, and have a job for security and certainty. You know when you'll get paid, have health insurance for yourself and your family, and can schedule things around that timeframe. I would guess that if you're reading this book, you may not be fulfilled in your job despite all the security it provides. You may think living this way is the "responsible" choice, especially because you're a parent and you need to provide for your family.

The W-2 job you equate to security is, in fact, the *least* secure option. While you get a predictable paycheck and insurance, you have no control over whether you stay employed. What if the economy shifts and the company you work for downsizes and lets you go? What if you're replaced by someone smarter, faster, or younger than you? Where does that leave you? What if technology makes your job obsolete?

You have no control over any of those scenarios. As a business owner, if any of those unknowns happen, you have all the control in the world. You can increase your own sales and marketing strategies. You can adjust your services to meet demand. You can change your branding to become attractive to a new clientele. As a business owner, you have all the options in the world to secure your future, rather than leaving it up to someone else to decide for you.

I'm actually surprised anybody wants a 9-5 job. It sounds awful!

Yet, despite all the "security" you have as a "W-2 parent," you still have this "itch" that won't go away, that lingers within you to discover, create and build. There are unutilized talents that you possess that are being wasted on the illusions of security and safety. You have much to contribute to this world and want to discover what that is. You sense there's more to experience in life than what you're currently living. But you pass potential opportunities by because your mind tells you that you don't have the spirit and mindset of an entrepreneur.

My dad and I once debated the "luck" factor in starting a business. He claimed I was very "lucky" to have the spirit that drives me to run my own business. Not everyone has that spirit, he claimed, or the will to create a business, even if they have a good idea. I debated with him for hours on this topic, but finally brought up something that happened during a family party.

My dad is a "W2 parent" with a business dream. He wanted a food truck company. During a family gathering, he expressed his dream of starting this business. The whole family got excited hearing his idea about this business venture. As he was talking, I was creating his business strategies in my head. But my aunt told me to not overwhelm him with those details yet.

"Get him to one farmer's market and just start selling," she said.

Unfortunately, he didn't take action and his dream of being a business owner stayed a dream.

So, when I brought up this scenario during our debate, I told him my passion for business had nothing to do with luck. My passion had been cultivated over years of self-discovery, failed businesses, and many lessons learned. I loved business because I finally figured out how I can succeed in it and have fun.

"Not all of us have that passion and energy to want to start our own businesses," he said. "It's too risky.".

"Passion and energy come when you have something to be passionate about," I said. "You had excitement, you shared the vision, and you didn't use it."

My dad didn't have a response to that. I called him out, but I didn't question why he didn't follow through.

I won't ask you why you won't start your business, but I will call you out on your curiosity. If you see my dad on the street, ask him about his food business venture. Especially if you are from the suburbs where he would clean house.

The Stay-At-Home Parent

Once I became a parent, I instinctually befriended other parents looking for support and advice. Frankly, I was looking for people to whom I could vent about my adorable, loveable, irritating, obnoxious, "spirited" son. Most of the time, I would share tales of how I would win the battle, yet somehow always feel like I was losing the war.

I had the privilege of talking to a new parent who was a stay-at-home parent, blessed with twin boys. She had been a stay-at-home parent for a few months, so I asked her why she decided not to go back to work. She told me that when it was time to go back, she realized that the cost of full-time daycare for two boys would roughly equal what she was making from her job. She concluded that it didn't make sense to return to a job where her entire paycheck would go towards someone else taking care of her kids.

After hearing her story, I couldn't help but think about how a small business might make so much sense for her if she desired to keep working and make a little extra money. I saw her desire to do something else besides just be a parent, but I also recognized her valid excuse of not having the energy.

Knowing this, I asked questions that revealed the solutions to her situation. How much time would she actually need to get a business up and running? And how can she find that time and energy within a given week? Answering those questions unlocked the solutions specific to her situation should she desire to have interest in starting a business. I shared these with her, but in her case, she wasn't ready. But something I said must have sunk in because, once her twins were older, she started not one but two businesses!

In certain situations, stay-at-home parents have made the decision to compromise a part of their lives in order to gain something else, whether it's time with their kids or minimizing expenses. You can, in fact, do it all: You can be with your kids, minimize expenses, chase your entrepreneurial dreams *and* make money. You can be at the water park while people are shopping in your online cart. You can make money while you are hanging out with your kids. And that doesn't look like dragging your kids to a job all weekend or on weeknights. They don't even know you're working half the time. In fact, you could debate that the best time to start a business is when your kids are young, for leveraging.

My wife told me about a mom who grew honey in her backyard. They lived in a house where the ground floor was the garage and the living floors were above it. My wife would simply ring the doorbell and be greeted by a 10-year-old boy who gave her the honey and collected the money. She heard his mom upstairs saying, "Sorry, I'm cooking right now. Thanks for your business."

Well played!

The mental line that stay-at-home parents need cross is: "Can I do it?" Some folks are ready sooner than others.

The Single Parent

I will forever have the utmost respect for single parents. The fact that you single-handedly manage your life along with that of a child (or children) is the stuff of legend. I have been privy to the challenges faced by single parents as I was raised by one.

My parents separated when I was in grade school, and I got to see firsthand how they handled it. As I was the setting the record for Most Difficult Adolescent to Raise, my parents took it in stride and managed to guide me while still living their individual lives. My dad taught me how to be responsible, live with integrity, and build personal character. My mom showed me how to adapt, adjust, and be a great entrepreneur.

My mom is one of the main reasons I'm a business owner today. If she enjoyed doing something, she would pursue it, and make money at it. For example, she loved to be around dogs so much that she created a dog-breeding business that evolved into a dog-showing business and placed at Eukanuba Dog Shows.

As long as I can remember, she was the purest example of an entrepreneurial spirit.

In high school, she juggled raising me, had a full-time job, ran a small software business, got her master's degree, and still managed to sleep ... all as a single parent. When I asked her how she did it, she said, "Sheer determination. I always kept my eyes on my goals. I also worked my ass off."

With all you've achieved as a single parent, if you're reading this book, there must be something within you telling you there's more out there for you. Is it a level of time you want to have, a level of flexibility in your schedule, a level of income, a level of fulfillment?

With kids, you are concerned about the energy, priorities, and time. I met a woman at business-mastery conference. She was a single parent, and told me she was a multi-millionaire making cakes from home. She started small. She converted her backyard patio into her office. People would simply walk through the back door to purchase her cakes. She had no real formal education. She just had to make it work. She knew she liked to make cakes, and had a talent for it. She hired someone to be the dishwasher, and others to do the jobs that would take her attention away from her culinary focus.

That dishwasher eventually became the person who made the dough, and now that person is the top designer. Having someone come in and do the tasks you don't enjoy will make you a happier business owner.

In all three scenarios, when contemplating a business, you will encounter some fear of incapability. Whether you're a parent or not, you can always find an excuse that would justify your inaction.

The Truth

I'm about to give you a bit of tough "parenting," but it's necessary to progress through the rest of this book and succeed. I want you to make an informed decision about starting a business. Whether you're working a W-2 job, a stay-at home parent, a single parent, or an empty-nest parent, here's a bit of insight when it comes to business:

Your Circumstances Will Not Dictate Your Success or Failure.

Circumstances are trivial. We all have 24 hours in a day, and we all have our individual hardships and challenges. We can always use the excuse that we don't have time because of our kids, or the economy isn't ready for my product, or that we are too tired after picking our kids up at school. The only thing that matters now is how you can get what you want based on your current circumstances. Rarely does the world align perfectly and fall into place.

As parents, we know that most of the time, our plans don't go our way, and we improvise, often with a few apologies ... but we have a vision of what we want to accomplish. If your purpose in starting a business matters to you, you will find a way.

We are inundated with the romance of being the business owner, although the truth of it is far from sexy. I wrote this book three days after my second son was born, and I was definitely *not* sexy when I showed up for my book coach.

So, what is one of the most common reasons why parents don't commit to starting a business? They're disillusioned, thinking they need to wait for the "right time" to start.

I connected with many parents and found out there is this illusion that the "stars have to align" for them to take action. Rarely do perfect circumstances come along for you to take action. And you have to admit, even if those "perfect circumstances" did come, it's a hard call whether you'd actually take action at that point because there has not been a full systematic vetting of the "reasons," i.e., fears.

The journey of my photography business was far from perfect or glamorous. The stars did not align, although a string of "unfortunate" events did shape the path to my business becoming a success. I also was able to define the "reasons" why I could not have formed the business and saw them as clearly many forms of fear. The fact is that nothing's more frightening than becoming a parent, no matter how many books you read or classes you take—yet we still do it!

I created my business while working a full-time job, and I had my best year in business around the birth of my son. If you find that your excuses are greater than your desires, then this book won't help. My desire is to help you move past your excuses and have some semblance of hope and possibility that you are capable of living your dreams, *especially* as a parent.

Over the years of mastering your parenting skills, you've unknowingly developed habits and strategies that work just as well in business as they do with your kids. This is not some elusive mystery, folks. It just takes the right steps and beliefs.

Chapter 3

Get Curious about Joy

"You can definitely find joy in business."

After all the people I've talked with, all the companies I've started, all the education I've absorbed, I've found there is only one reason why any of us consider starting a business. Under all the vision, mission statements, marketing strategies, networking, sales, and business jargon, we as parents and as individuals create businesses for one reason. It's a reason similar to why children do anything: JOY.

The word "joy" encapsulates many feelings, such as fulfillment, contribution, achievement, fun, love, happiness, understanding, security, variety, growth, connection, acceptance, and so on. The concept of "joy" can be found in many ways: Having more free time, building a connection with clients, getting smiles for doing a great job, earning more money, having a sense of "taking control," teaching others, learning and applying our education, or inventing new ways of doing things. We are constantly searching for joy and might have decided to look for it in our own businesses. And speaking from my own experience, I say that you can definitely find joy in business.

No matter how much you try to suppress that curiosity, your gifts will always shine and continually nag you to address the wonder of possibility. And here's the best part of giving it a try: Ultimately, you can't lose!

Let's say you start your business, and it succeeds. You win. Now let's say you start your business, and you don't like it. You decide it's not for you. Congratulations, you win again! The itch has been scratched and will no longer itch. You won't wonder "what if," and spend time daydreaming about running a business. You'll have experienced it and moved on.

My interest in photography first emerged in 2009. I was working a traditional 9-5 job, lived pretty stable with my life but had an ache for more. I was searching. Numerous big businesses were closing down due to the downturn in the economy, and an electronic store called Circuit City was liquidating in my area. My girlfriend (who became my wife) and I decided to head over and see if there was anything on sale that we wanted.

The store was pretty emptied of inventory. On one of the display tables, I saw this large, bulky camera. I picked it up, looked through the viewfinder at my girlfriend and said, "Smile!"

One click was all it took. I was hooked! Taking a photo felt "right" to me. Excited to explore more, I *got* curious. I researched cameras online, asked my photographer-friends about their craft, and talked to salespeople at specialty camera stores about all things photography. I looked at every brand, every camera body, all the classes I could take, and all the options available to me. I was obsessed. I couldn't stop thinking about buying my first camera.

After I bought a camera, I learned about photography art and technique from the schools of Google and YouTube. I searched every other keyword and looked at every free video tutorial about photography. I was immersing myself, learning the mystic arts of post-processing, control of lighting, and about angles. If there is a free online video on photography, chances are I've seen it. While gathering all that data, I started to experiment and practice what I learned.

I photographed everything I could—family events, nature, our travels, monuments, and my girlfriend (who hated me photographing her). I would go to my network and ask if I could photograph them for free. My camera was now part of my wardrobe. As sure as I would put on my shoes, I had a camera around my neck.

I also shared some of my best work at the time online. I showed my friends all my photos, hoping they'd like them and told them I was doing photography on the side. I was feeling joy and, for me at least, is all that's required to be in business. I'm crazy that way!

In the beginning of my photography journey, one of my mentors quickly saw what was going on with my evolution as a photographer and had a chat with me. He had been working with me for a long time and knew exactly what I was thinking and where I was going.

"Jeremy, I'm very happy that you have found this new hobby of yours," he told me. "Do *not* make it a business—yet."

I gasped. "How did you know I wanted to start a business?" I began. "And why would you tell me not to? I'm having so much fun. Why wouldn't I try to make money doing something that I love? Isn't that the point of starting a small business?"

He smiled and said, "You're exactly right. You should always try to make money doing what you love. But you're not ready yet. Keep doing your photography, but here's the key: Focus on having fun. Keep having fun and watch what happens."

This mentor was helping me walk, and reminding me I didn't need to sprint yet.

I was in my joy, and that was apparent. He was cautioning me if I moved too fast, I would bump up against all the fears and issues that could shut me down before I even started.

One of my serial entrepreneur friends gave me my first photography job. He knew I had a camera and was doing photography as a hobby. He was launching a baby product line and asked if I could help him take photos of the product and some baby "models" to go with the product. He knew I was still new at this so he assured me that he would direct everything and plan everything out, from how to light the set to what angles to take. I agreed.

During breaks in the photo session, I took photos of the two "models," who couldn't have been more than two and four years old. After the session, I gave my friend the photos and said their parents could have them. He scrolled through the photos. He looked at me and said, "Jeremy, you will not understand what I'm about to tell you. One day, you will be a full-time photographer."

Completely shocked, I responded, "What do you mean?"

"You were able to capture the essence of these kids with your photography," he said. "You have a talent for it. Keep doing what you're doing, and there is no doubt you'll be a full-time photographer".

From that moment on, I focused on photographing people, weddings, birthday parties, headshots to business branding photography. I took them all, knowing I'd learn more and build a portfolio. And with all these requests, I started to get paid for my services! No business plan was made, no goals or benchmarks defined, and no vision to guide me other than my passion and naïve curiosity. I just had fun and eventually started making money doing what I enjoyed doing.

Identify Your Fears

I love to hear parents talk about their "great ideas" for a business, and then push them beyond their comfort zones. I'll usually dig for information to find out why they haven't started their journey. I hear all the fears preventing them from committing. Remarkably, no matter their individual circumstances, I notice a similarity in their reasons, and that's fear. All "reasons" stem from fear, and their fear prevents them from taking action.

The unknown is scary especially when you begin intellectualizing it as you would a business.

Fear can creep up on us if we don't pay attention, especially when it is generalized. It can paralyze us or push us forward. I would like to articulate that fear isn't necessarily negative or inherently "bad." It can indicate we are taking action or preparing to take action.

That is why understanding our specific fears to starting a business as a parent is helpful before moving forward. As I've talked with countless parents, I see a reoccurring pattern of undefined fears that repeat themselves despite the parents' circumstances, whether they're a single parent, stay at home parent, etc. They don't call them fears, however. They call them "reasons." Based on my conversations, these are the top "reasons" why many parents haven't started their own business (even when they have a great idea):

> *Reason #1: I don't want to fail.* (Fear of Failure)

> *Reason #2: I don't have the resources to start a business. (Fear of Lack)*

> *Reason #3: I have no time or energy. (Fear of Fallibility)*

> *Reason #4: I'm comfortable with how things are. I have a stable job, income, health insurance, etc. Why would I risk that to start a business, which is full of risk? (Fear of the Unknown)*

You must acknowledge your concerns/fears and address them specifically so you can explore the possibilities of what you can create and achieve within your business. People don't realize how much courage it takes to be positive. That courage comes from addressing these reasons head-on and finding solutions that help you move forward with your business idea.

Reason #1: Failure

There is this cloud of doubt that comes over parents and potential business owners when thinking about trying something new—especially something as "big" as starting a business. They think about everything that can go wrong, question whether they could even succeed, and debate whether their idea would work. They question whether they could make money executing on their idea and whether it's sustainable for their lifestyle. All this doubt might have merit; past failures could validate their lack of confidence. They've tried new activities, weren't good at it, so they digressed and dared not to try anything too risky again.

You are setting the bar way too high in the beginning. Your

visions for your business might be the "end goals" you're aspiring to—and you're just starting out. You hear about businesses that become "overnight successes" but don't see the years it took to become that "overnight success." It's like your toddler running a marathon before taking his or her first steps.

As adults, our courage is diluted by too much pressure from expectations in the beginning. So, it's obvious why you wouldn't want to start. And even if you did start, with such an unreasonably high bar already set, you would most likely give up after you've run into your first obstacle.

Solution #1: Set yourself up to win

GREAT NEWS! The solution is actually quite simple: Set yourself up to win. When teaching a child how to walk, we don't expect them to start walking right away. The first goal is to get them crawling. Once they are strong enough to lift their head and support their upper body with their arms, they realize they can move around. Next is to get them excited about standing up. Once they're up, we encourage them to take a step forward toward you. They will fall, but they will get back up. They will fall again, and get back up. You repeat this process until the exciting day when they take their first step towards you! SUCCESS ... until they fall down again.

This process all started with simple steps. We didn't start with them walking, running marathons or obstacle course races. We started with where they were at and focused on the next step. And the same strategy can be applied with you starting a business.

If you're brand-new to starting a business and the fear of failure is one of your reasons why you haven't started yet, act like your two-year-old. Your focus is on seeing what you can do and trying out new things. Your "job" at this point is to experience, learn, explore. And as we stated earlier, your goal right now is to find your joy. That's it. It's not about accounting, sales and marketing, human resources, CRM, SEO, or any business jargon. Your job is to figure out what you enjoy and why you enjoy it.

Reason #2: Resources

The second reason parents use to not start their business is the perception that they lack resources. Money, expertise, connections, or support. I hear statements like, "It takes money to make money," and "I don't have any so how can I start a business," or "I never got a business degree, so I don't know how to start a business." People also tell me how they don't have the contacts to getting their businesses off the ground or the support from their friends and family. All of these statements may be true, but a lack of resources is rarely the real reason for not getting started.

Have you ever watched your child process challenges? They never seem to worry about having a lack of resources. I watched my two-year-old son attempt to climb a chair, focused on the task at hand. He never complains about not being tall enough or not strong enough to achieve the task. If anything, I'm the "voice of reason" telling him he can't climb the chair in fear that he could fall and hurt himself. Sure enough, with enough effort and persistence, he climbs the chair.

I look at my interactions with my son and realize how much I limit his abilities with my "protective" voice. My fear of him "failing" (i.e., making a mess or hurting himself) creates this controlling parent constantly telling him he "can't" do the thing he wants to do, like walk upstairs without my assistance, feed himself, or carry around a cup of watercolors.

Fortunately, I married a very smart person who knows that cultivating our son's curiosity and desire to problem-solve are crucial for his development. So, she limits my "voice of reason" and lets him explore his capabilities.

We were all born with the desires to explore our potential, regardless of our resources. Over time, we have been bombarded with rules and "cannots" in the form of guidance and love from those we were raised by. Although their intentions were good in giving us their guidance, their lifetime of influence has created these limiting beliefs—and these come into play as you balk at the thought of starting a business. Understand that your "lack" of resources does not have authority or power over your ability to problem-solve your way to success.

Solution #2: Get resourceful

When I was young, I told myself I didn't want to start a family until I knew I could financially support one. My wife's pregnancy meant I was looking at a nine-month ticking clock without a job and a photography business. I didn't have the time to worry about whether I went to the best photography school or had enough savings. I already had the best resource available—the problem-solving mentality I'd already honed as a child. That, combined with the second best resource around— the internet—I was unstoppable.

I made a list of all the weak spots within my business: no studio location, no consistent marketing strategies, no marketable photography skill set, and no idea what to do next. I talked to my network of my friends/family and asked for help with my website, logo, and business cards. I went online and researched every marketing avenue that fit my non-existent budget. I looked at every viable studio space that I could afford. I learned all the photography techniques I could gain access to through video tutorials and photo blogs. In short, I became resourceful.

After you develop your resourceful self, understand the one tremendous tool you have access to on your phone or laptop: the internet. The internet makes this the best time in history to start a business. The internet has created a more level playing field for all entrepreneurs, especially new ones. You have access to the education needed to start up virtually any type of business, if you know how to search for it. You have access to a worldwide network of specialists. You can also find communities to support you in your endeavors, should you desire such help and assistance. In this day and age, it's virtually impossible to NOT get started on a business because technology has made it so "turn-key" and accessible.

Look at how resourceful you are as a parent every time you have a puzzling challenge with your child. When my wife and I had our son, we noticed how his speech was a bit "behind" compared to our friends' kids. (It's funny how we will always compare our kids to others.) We were a bit concerned because we didn't want him to be behind when he went to school but didn't know what we needed to do. Our friends and family gave tips like, "Talk to your son as if you're a sportscaster, not a psychologist," or "Talk to him using statements rather than asking him questions." My wife searched online for any resources that were available to us to get him started. She found options for speech therapists, which we ended up hiring. The therapist helped us by showing activities to do with our son that promoted talking. With all our resourcefulness, we now have a child that talks … and talks … and talks … and talks. Now I wonder if we should have waited a while longer to start that process so we could have had a few more moments of peace!

Apply what we did for my kids to your business. Ask yourself what resources you already have and what resources you think you need. Find forums, communities on social media, tips online, experts, and peers that might help you. Talk about how you're considering starting a business and state what you're looking for. Don't be afraid to ask. If you don't ask, the answer will be no 100% of the time. And realize that just by being a parent, you are more "educated" in running a business than you think.

Reason #3: Time

It's obvious that time is a huge factor when considering any activities, especially for parents. As a father, finding a moment without my son asking me to do something for him is a miracle. "I'm going to the bathroom" is sometimes the best ploy for getting some "alone time" (and it still doesn't always work). Yes, I wrote some of my book there. TMI?

Time tends to be blur as a parent, so it's logical to reason that adding another project (like starting a business) would use up time you don't even have. You're thinking, Jeremy: Are you actually suggesting I start a business amidst getting my kids ready for school, taking them to school, cleaning the house, doing laundry, buying groceries, taking the dog out for a walk, parent/teacher conferences, cheering on after-school activities, paying attention to my spouse, finding personal alone-time, reading updates on social media, catching up on my weekly shows, making dinner, and putting my kids to bed?

Yes, I am. Because you actually get more time when you start a business as a parent. It's counter-intuitive, but I am living proof of it's true, and I believe it so much that I even had a second kid as a business owner AND wrote this book three days after he was born.

Responsible parents do a great job with all the responsibilities they carry. By default, they become excellent time managers, whether they're elegant about it or not. They manage to get so much done in a 24-hour day, although there might be days when it seems like you didn't get anything done. And because of that focus and commitment, I believe that you are more than capable of starting your own business.

Solution #3: The time you need is less than you think.

If you've never started a business before and are considering starting one, the time you use towards launching this process is surprisingly small. What if I were to tell you that all you would need is about four hours per week? Is it possible for you to find four hours in any given week to devote to your business? If you were committed, could you find four hours a week?

I can hear what you're saying: "What could I possibly get done with four hours a week? It will take forever to get my business running. Why even start?"

Well, I'm glad you asked. If the time seems so insignificant, then you shouldn't have a problem finding the time for this exercise. The important thing is to get started. The amount of time you need is trivial. Action beats inaction any day. The time you "need" is less important than the time you commit to action.

Reason #4: Why Rock the Boat

The last reason I hear about why parents don't start a business is because they're comfortable with their lifestyle. They can anticipate the stress they are going to walk into. They have a gnawing ache but think they are being frivolous or unreasonable. Many parents have created what I call the "textbook" lifestyle. They have a house, a secure job that they're good at, security with a steady paycheck and health insurance for their family, and a stable daily routine. They reached the level of success that they've always aspired to within the company they work for. Why would they want to risk all of that to start a business?

To these parents, a business equals stress and hardship, with highs and lows. With a business, you start at the bottom, working your way up to the top. If you already had to do that with your current 9-5 job, why would you want to go through that again? Again, you're playing out the tape far too long into the future, sabotaging your present desire. What if I hire people for my business who then rely on me to feed their families, and I fail, and now I have to fire them? What if my business does succeed, and I'm working 24/7, and I no longer get time with my family, and they all hate me?

Why can't I just be satisfied with the life I have, and stop having all these ridiculous annoying visions and dreams of a business?

Solution #4: Why not have both?

I'm here to promote that *even if* you have all the above reasons/fears, and you're *still* curious about starting a business, you're seeking more fulfillment in your life, and you have the gumption and courage to get it. You're curious about what else you can accomplish in this life. You're curious about what it might be like to experience running your own business. You're intrigued by reaching another level.

Many parents think that starting a business means they need to quit their job tomorrow and start "the business." Why have either/or when you can have both? Just as a two-year-old tries new foods, you can experiment with new talents. There are some foods a toddler will like, some he won't. If you're trying to get your child to try a variety of foods, what do you do? For one, you check in with other parents and see what their strategies are. So, instead of experiencing a business all on your own, you should connect and hang out with other business owners on the weekends.

It's time to explore what "might be" once and for all. If you have that lingering annoyance in your professional life that you can't explain, try something new: Test your limitations. See what else life has to offer.

Do research about the need for your business in your area. Check out the competition. Do a free session or service for someone. You buy small bites for your kid and see what he likes and doesn't like. In this process of exploring the entrepreneurial world, you too are taking small bites and distinguishing what you like and don't like. Only then will you know whether a business has the potential to bring you joy or not. Whether it's running your own business or having a child, these events are here to help us learn more about ourselves and help us develop into the people we desire to be.

The truth is there is no better time to start a business than today. With the access the internet provides, you have a global network of resources at your disposal. You just need to take action, and get it started.

And I'll tell you again, the fact that you are a parent gives you more business experience that you think. Most parents are better equipped to start a business than a fresh-out-of-college business graduate who isn't a parent.

The psychology of a parent makes you well-prepared to being a business owner. It helped me make more money (as a parent) with a business than my whole career before I had my first child (even when I had a traditional job).

First, I stayed with my joy, and put in my four hours a week. When the business picked up, I fought the fears and continued to invest more time and resources.

My son was born in May 2015. By the end of 2016, I had generated over six figures in revenue. It was more than I ever had made in any business OR at a W-2 job. I worked two days less a week, and I more than doubled my income.

So, if someone tells me they don't start a business as a parent because of time or resources, I say bullshit. I had neither—until I made the decision to have both.

Chapter 4

Exploring the World of Your Business

"Your initial hours: Where it all begins."

In chapter three, I outlined the three biggest fear obstacles for potential business owners (you) and offered tangible solutions. I may have even convinced you that your inner chatter of doubt can be surmounted. Next, I suggested you may only need to devote four hours a week to start your business. Did you eye-roll? Or did you miss that point completely? I'm going to emphasize that fundamental belief now so don't toss the book on the couch and glare at it.

Laying the foundation of internal awareness, and getting clear about your desires about starting a business: These are crucial times you will look back on one day as the core actions that precede the business starting.

It's the "getting to the gym" syndrome. The hardest part about getting to the gym is ... getting to the gym. The strategy to getting your results may not be glamorous or groundbreaking. Stating the idea that working on your business doesn't involve a heap of time is not a bold claim. I will get bolder with my advice, trust me, but for now, let's explore what you can accomplish in this valuable but brief time.

I stated that you can start your journey with a minimum of four hours a week, yet the number of hours is irrelevant. Because once you dive into that first hour, you'll be off and running. You'll build momentum and ten hours later, you'll want to do it again tomorrow.

The objective is to take action. Whether you invest 10 minutes or 10 hours, ACTION is what brings real results, and action builds on action once it starts. One action will lead to another and another until one day, you realize that you are what you have always wanted to be: a business owner.

If these statements are true, the next obvious question would be: *What do I do with my initial time investment?*

For starters, don't make the initial hours precious. That is one of the surest ways to killing your business before it even starts. Please don't put pressure on yourself. These initial hours are actually **your** time to explore and enjoy, independent of your family, friends, circumstances, excuses, and responsibilities.

This time is for you to learn about what makes your idea attractive to you, where you start to find your JOY, and explore why you like your business idea in the first place.

Apprehension will be part of this equation. The first foray into even minor exploration can be daunting and comparable to taking your first trip to the store with your newborn. You choose a store within a three-mile proximity in case you forgot something (like the refrigerator). You pack an army rucksack, not worrying about how much it weighs and over-bundle your child. The trip is set for a time of day when the store won't be too crowded, reducing the chances of your child being coughed or sneezed on.

Regardless of these obsessive measures, you accomplish your mission, Operation Protect the Baby, and you make it home that much more knowledgeable about what you do or don't have to do next time.

The initial voyage of your business mothership is very similar. Although you may not be carrying a rucksack of supplies, you may overcomplicate the simplicity of finding joy. The good news is that cautionary measures will keep you alert about finding the most useful resources for completing your objectives.

Imagination

What makes you want to begin imagining your business most? The creative element? The efficiency of how a business generates revenue? Or the innovation of how the business will change the world? The awareness of your unique desire is key to setting up how you approach your business on a day-to-day basis.

Whether in your head, on a piece of paper, or using the notepad or recorder app on your phone, envision what your business will look like when built up to 100% in some or all these areas. Do this before you launch anything.

A business has many moving parts, and a lot of roles to fill. Where do you see yourself working in the business? What do you see yourself doing on a day-to-day basis where you'll be enjoying the process and feeling fulfilled? Do you see yourself "on the front line" talking with customers and managing a team of employees? Are you "behind the scenes" creating your product, while others do the sales and marketing? Are you the strategic planner that creates systems within your business, the one in charge of the overall vision and direction of the company? What vision excites you?

Okay, okay! System overload. Don't let these questions put too much pressure on you during this imagination phase. Give yourself some slack and relax. If you have never started a business before, these key questions will help provide a framework within which your mind can wander. Take note of what shows up. As a two-year-old is programmed to search for joy, you have the same capacity if you simply let go of being perfect and just be. The answers will come.

Creativity is key here even if you don't consider yourself a creative person. You don't have to be a slam poet or a fashion designer to exercise your entrepreneurial imagination and conceive the ideal scenario for your business.

Be wary of the intrusions of the outside world in this creative and imaginative time. People think they "mean well," but they can squash your dream.

When I started photography, I envisioned creating a six-figure annual income, knowing I had never before reached that fiscal goal. I told a friend (who was a serial entrepreneur) of my aspiration, and he cautioned me to "be realistic," to consider my history of failed businesses and lack of experience. I had another established photographer-friend tell me I couldn't make six figures because my photography wasn't good enough to generate that level of revenue.

Even with their "good opinions" waged against me, I still dared to dream and imagine what life would be like when I did achieve my photography goals. I am so happy I didn't listen to them because I became that six-figure photographer and started just as I am instructing you to do. (I'll get into the pitfalls of "good advice" later in this chapter.). Have the faith of a two-year-old and just dream of possibilities, no matter how quixotic. These initial hours are for you and you alone to discover what might be possible. The last thing you need is "good advice."

Observation

Once you have an idea about what your business is (you can even give yourself a fantastic fun title like Chief Dada), you can start researching it. Educate yourself and observe comparable companies with a critical eye. Look at what other companies are doing right, and adopt those strategies and techniques. Look at how they sell their products or services. How do you feel about their methods and approach?

We all have experiences all day long as consumers. Start to notice what brands stand out to you and why. If you think you could do better than a given brand, what would you do differently? Also observe companies outside your industry, critiquing what they do and their effectiveness. Notice the little details of an experience, such as a hand-written thank-you note on a receipt, package and pricing strategies on a menu, or how quickly a product was shipped to you.

Making these observations will help you as you create your personal brand, distinguishing why your business is unique compared to other companies in your industry.

A business can be a self-expression of values and beliefs with an owner. You can see very quickly what a brand IS and IS NOT by how they interact with others. You will notice if they value efficiency, customer service, long-term relationships, maximizing a sale, etc. Studying companies that are aligned with your tastes and values provides even deeper insight into the type of clientele you would want to serve.

Notice how I'm not using the term word "competitors" when talking about companies to observe. You are not in that game yet. You are still exploring the possibilities of business. Every decision you make is very new and is subject to change (like a two-year-old's attention span). Identifying competitors is futile at this point and may be a disservice to you because you can feel disillusioned and silly in contemplating getting in the ring with established companies.

Community

One powerful resource I have found invaluable in business (and in parenting) is the power of community. Within your four allotted hours, look for people in your network and community who own businesses or used to own businesses and ask a lot of questions. Grill them. They are the best business coaches you can get. They are free, and they're in the midst of it! Also, look for individuals or groups that have business backgrounds or skills that might pertain directly to your business concept. Take what you like and leave the rest. Don't be too picky about who they are or their level of expertise and success—yet. Your job is to become resourceful and see where help may be found.

If you find you don't know many people or have much support, start looking outside your personal network. Online social media sites have communities established for general businesses support, industry-specific businesses networking, and business education. A lot of these communities are free to join and can provide you with much insight into the day-to-day activities of a business owner. These communities are also a great way to connect with others in your industry and learn. Reach out to them individually, tell them that you're thinking of starting a business, and ask them questions about their experiences.

People love to talk about themselves, especially business owners! Ask them how they got started, and you might find yourself captive to a 15-minute signature speech. Glean from their trajectory what to expect.

If you don't feel comfortable reaching out to people online, try the direct approach. If your network of friends and family have never started businesses before, ask them if they know someone who has. They might be able to refer or connect you to business owners who might help.

You can also try the community route in your local area. Local communities have tons of activities where you can reach out to others. Join "common interest groups" like book clubs, cooking classes, or children's activities. While there, make new friends and get to know them. You never know who you'll meet, and how they might be able to help you build your business.

If any of those options don't work for you in terms of resources, use ME as a resource! I love helping others fulfill their dreams and would love to help where I can. I am completely serious. I give out my email at the end of this book.

I'm offering free advice, and here is the funny part. About 1% of people will take me up on that offer. People are scared to take a leap, but as this is part of your exploration, you have nothing to lose when anyone offers to answer an email or take a call from you for advice. Sure, there are people who will try to upsell you a coaching program or product. You will learn to politely decline, especially in this early phase of your business.

We will get to enlisting paid help later in the book. The point right now is to cull together the free resources you have at your disposal and start leveraging them for success. As you grow, you will position yourself to help others and "pay it forward."

As you dedicate time to your initial weekly hours, you should be mindful that the road ahead will be littered with inevitable mistakes, old habits, unfavorable luck, or errors in judgment, all of which can deter your progress. You may be fortunate and not experience any roadblocks, but you should be prepared to address them in the unlikely event that any (or all) of these occur.

Roadblocks aren't inherently "bad" either; they're part of the process and should be acknowledged. Let's look at five key conditions for you to look out for, and if you find yourself locked into one, be kind to yourself, acknowledge what happened, address the situation, and get back on course.

1. Wrong Focus

The #1 mistake people make when they start their own business from scratch is focusing on marketing that doesn't matter much in the beginning, specifically deciding on the name of the company, the logo design, creating full-fledged website, writing copy, getting their social media sites up and their profiles created, and ordering business cards and flyers. When someone gets excited to start a business, their focus in creating an actual business can get steered away by creating a business *persona*. After countless hours and resources put into these tasks (including the lovely initial hours set aside for imaginative exploration), they have a business brand … with no business sales or marketing in place.

I intend to help you focus on creating the "why" of the actual business—which exists to attract the ideal customers—not the perception of being a business owner. If you focus solely on perception, the messaging will come forth as forced and not from an authentic place.

The reason why people tend to focus on these tasks first is because they provide you with "busy work." They fill up your time, giving you the illusion that you're being productive and that you're moving forward with your business. While these tasks will be crucial at some point, they're not needed in the very beginning of your business, especially if you've never started one before. When I started my photography business, I spent tons of time creating several designs of business cards, ordered 1,000 of them only to decide on a different style three months later. My logo went through four revisions within the first six months. I created the website, established the social media accounts, and was ready for business!

No one knocked on my door. The phones didn't ring. The email box was empty. No one knew I existed. The business was "made," but I'd spent no time marketing or selling the service. So, I was yet another great business idea that no one knew about.

Your initial focus is to have fun or search for your joy. This is your time to explore and get to know yourself better as a creator. Fear may come. Doubt may come. Both are perfectly normal emotions to feel and signs that you're exploring beyond your comfort zones, but don't let them derail you. Acknowledge the feelings and stay focused during these initial hours getting educated. I can guarantee you that the more time you spend really understanding how you will be of service to your clients/customers, the less holes there will be to plug a year or two down the road.

2. Afraid to ask for help

When my wife and I found out we were pregnant, my mother-in-law was so excited. She said she wanted to help as much as she could, changing the baby, giving us breaks to sleep, and being there for whatever we needed. My ego told her, "Don't worry about us. We can take handle everything. You don't need to help us out. We are more than capable of raising our baby by ourselves." Luckily, she wasn't interested in getting my permission. And thank goodness for that!

After just the three weeks of crying, diaper changes, sleep deprivation, two-hour feeding cycles, and non-stop "white noise" in the background, I was at my wits' end and couldn't wait for my mother-in-law's arrival. She would take him, and I would run straight to my bed, lock the door, and pass out until my body decided to get up again. Those moments made me realize how asking for help as a parent is as important as it is for a new business owner. If someone offers to help, accept it (especially in the beginning).

When I was managing the life of being a parent and running a photography business, there were instances where projects were scheduled on days I was watching my son. I turned down most of them, but one had such an upside that I struggled with saying no.

Venting to a friend, I told her how frustrated I was and how this project would be a great opportunity for future work with the company, but I had no one to watch my son. Wanting to help, she offered to volunteer her time to watch him while I did the photo shoot. Feeling bad for being an inconvenience, I politely declined her generous offer and told her I would have to miss the opportunity and wait for the next one. Seeing how conflicted I was with the situation, she wouldn't take "no" for an answer and told me to take the job. Fortunately, she used to be a nanny, so she had a lot of experience with kids. I said yes.

When starting your business, don't be afraid to ask for help. You may not want to ask, in fear that you could be inconveniencing others or burdening them with your ventures, but as "it takes a village to raise a child," your business will need similar attention.

Here's a secret that a friend told me: If you're starting a new business and taking care of your kids simultaneously, share that with others, and see what happens. I have found that when I tell people about raising a toddler while running my business full-time, they're invariably accommodating and/or willing to help, however they can. The lesson here is to accept the goodwill with gratitude and keep going. You will never hear me say that I'm a "self-made" businessman," because I'm aware of all the people who've supported me throughout my entire journey, whether they be friends, family, clients, or colleagues. As the saying goes, "If you never ask for help, the answer 100% of the time will be 'no'."

3. Comparison

One of the biggest traps business owners can fall into in starting a business is comparing themselves to others. I've been guilty of this too many times (and still find myself doing it today). While I suggest you scope out what other companies in your industry are doing, you don't need to parrot their look, style, or business model. In this phase, as you continue to look at comparisons of what "could be" for your company, don't compare your humble beginnings with what you perceive as their success, especially when they appear to have "never" made a mistake. You will get discouraged to start. You're not seeing what they invested and powered through to get their business to that impressive level of success. Their success is nothing more than a byproduct of the decisions, actions, failures, and successes they had to endure during the lifecycle of their business. Yours will be the same.

I mentioned how my son had a speech "delay" when he was two years old, that is, he wasn't speaking the "standard" range of words he "should" be at his age. I was having a hard time with this, thinking I was a bad parent for not taking the right actions to get him to speak more words. What didn't help was seeing our friends' kids (who were the same age as my son) speaking very well, learning at what seemed to be a more rapid pace, and communicating with their parents extremely well. This compounded my feelings of inadequacy as a parent and made me feel like a failure.

What I failed to mention was that my friends (whose kids were practically scholars at two years old) had worked in the child-development field (along with some of their immediate family). So, their training naturally kicked in and produced remarkable results in their children's speech and "advanced" results.

Once I stopped comparing, I was able to research the help my son needed. As I mentioned before, now he won't shut up. So, build your business for the ideal clients, and, when free from the trap of comparison and self-doubt, know that they will come. You will be busy!

As I accepted that my son has his own evolution of success, you must accept that your business will have an evolution of its own. You must honor where you are in your business and trust that you can get the results you desire in time. Your timeline is yours, and you are unique to your business.

4. Noise

As I have encouraged you to ask for help in building your business, I also need to warn you of the pitfalls in the "good opinion of other people." Often, the advice you are given is based on someone's prior conditioning, not on your unique situation and desires. These well-intended folks will give advice about what you "should" do and what you "shouldn't" do, even when they have no experience in the subject matter.

These people are often in your immediate circle. The "shoulds" can show up from family members, close friends, or anyone you may hold dear to you. Most of the time, they come from a good place, wanting to make sure you succeed. However, their advice may not be grounded by experience or expertise, but by what they heard from others or what they had envisioned for themselves but never followed through on. This means that their advice is anything but. It is noise to distract you from your joy and your own why.

As you are in the very delicate phase of imagination and exploration in your business, steer clear of almost all noise (aside from my book of course, because I would never steer you wrong.)

The way you spot these "good opinions" is very simple: If their advice comes before you articulate to them what you desire, beware. Usually, they will hear that you're starting a business and immediately want to tell you what you "should" or "shouldn't" do, without ever hearing what you want to create. I'm not saying that their advice may not be accurate or good advice, but more often than not, their advice won't be appropriate for you without proper screening.

Should you find yourself with someone inquisitive and seemingly helpful, who could potentially have some good advice based on their experience, you can direct the conversation by asking specific questions instead of broad ones. Instead of asking, "What marketing should I do?" ask, "If I wanted to sell my product to working millennials who love to surf, where would I find them?" That way, you clarify your needs and can decipher whether the advice you're given fits the criteria of what information you're searching for.

As a parent, I used to hear advice from relatives about what I "should" and "shouldn't" do in raising my son. The advice doesn't stop there. Articles and opinions are all over my social-media feeds about the "shoulds" and "shouldn'ts," based on these studies or that anecdotal experience.

At some point, all the access to this data just becomes noise. I finally started becoming aware and changed my approach with harvesting data. I focused on the outcome I desired with my son's speech development and screened data from that filter. That way, I figured out if the information I was given aligned with my desires and evaluated whether or not I wanted to apply the information.

5. Tomorrow Syndrome

Dedicating your initial four hours a week to starting a business may seem trivial and irrelevant. This strategy may sound so simplistic that you find yourself putting this commitment off until "tomorrow" or "later." Usually, this occurs when the desire to begin and/or the belief in your abilities are weak. Deep down, you may feel some anticipation of disappointment that you don't want to experience, so you put off the task to another time. You think, it's just four hours. I can fit that in anytime. Then you never do.

The solution is simple: Act like a two-year-old!

Have you ever asked a two-year-old to wait for something? How did that work out for you? My son loves the concept of NOW. He'll come up to me, ask if he can have candy, to which I will respond with a "later, after you eat lunch." Five seconds later, he'll ask the same question. My will is firm, and my answer repeats. After 20 repeated attempts in less than a minute, my "firm" will has now slowly crumbled away, and I give him whatever he wants.

As kids love the concept of NOW, so should you. Tomorrow never comes, so "when would NOW be a good time"? This is why, in the exploration phase of your business journey, your goal is to find your joy; when you schedule your four hours, you need to be in that NOW.

Get excited about scheduling your four hours. Treat it like a dream vacation that you get to experience every week. Eventually, on one of those vacations, a big lightbulb will go off, and you will have "the idea." Waste no time, write it down, post-its are fantastic ways to capture dreams that become realities. While four hours is not enough time to fully explore the many facets of running your future business, they'll get you to take action by showing up. You'll be able to officially say that you are "Parenting A Business."

Chapter 5

Jumping From the Four Hours

"Persistence is your greatest weapon."

You are back for chapter five, which indicates you are either a glutton for punishment or you actually want more information about parenting a business. In some ways, it will always be both with parenting and business ownership, but the rewards are innumerable in either case. Do you recall what it's like to get a butterfly kiss from your kid, or to tickle them? That is what it also feels like to get your first sale.

Whether you put the four initial hours into your exploration process, or two weeks, or 30 minutes, the end goal is to discover anything you might love to do in your vision of a business. That spark or hint of joy will make time will fly by, and you will want to work on your business day and night. When I first started learning about photography, I couldn't stop thinking about taking photos or wanting to learn more about my craft. Every spare moment I had went into the pursuit of bettering myself within photography, even to the neglect of my wife from time to time. OOPS! Yeah, I was obsessed. I felt like I'd "caught the bug," and my entire focus became about this one craft.

Originally, I was attracted to network marketing companies because they seemed like it an ideal fit for my skill set. I'd successfully created five **failed** businesses to hone in on that inner voice, the one that told me my photography business would be the one to have the longevity and produce the most joy.

I always looked for something that matched my natural talents, but I never felt like I got much value of those marketing companies. The business model seemed like a perfect fit, but I was not yet in my Joy, so they failed every time.

You can start with what seems obvious to do as a business, and you may find it on the first try. If your journey is destined to have a detour route, like mine did, keep going! Your persistence is your greatest weapon.

To build up the right kind of momentum for your discovery process, take an idea or two as to what type of business you want to create, and what type of joy you wish to experience within the business, and match it to these three key actions.

1. Focus In: What You Love

Looking at your idea for a product or service, I'm sure most of you will want to join an industry with a lot of people already doing what you want to do. When I started my photography business, I felt like photography was the most oversaturated industry out there, due to the advancement in technology, which enabled anyone to buy a camera and take an amazing photo. Phones were also integrating camera technology with hardware that was comparable to my "professional" equipment. This advancement made anyone with a phone a "photographer." One of the best pieces of advice, though it might sound intimidating or limiting in the beginning of your business development, is *focus in.* That is, focus in on what the business's value is and who specifically would benefit. Another way to focus in is by answering a question: Where would you find the most joy if you were to eliminate all the factors/people you didn't want to interact with?

After I decided to explore photography as a hobby and bought my first camera, my wife and I went on a trip to Paris, France. Naturally, I brought my camera. I was really excited to take photos there. I snapped shots of the Eiffel Tower, the Arc de Triomphe, Notre-Dame, and so much more.

Something interesting happened when I took all those photos. I was completely bored! I couldn't stand walking around with a camera/tripod, put on a few settings, take a couple of photos, and move on. That process wasn't fun. I tried that process a few more times back home, photographing San Francisco City Hall at night and the Golden Gate Bridge. Still bored. (Note to self: If what I'm photographing doesn't speak to me, I won't enjoy photographing it. Good to know.)

The purpose of focusing in is two-fold. While it is part of finding the angle of your business, it's also narrowing down the field of your product or service so people can effortlessly make referrals to you.

You also want to know what kind of customers you want to attract to your business. Life is short. Get as specific as possible from the get-go, and you can make adjustments to your marketing later on. You may discover that your conception of an ideal client isn't accurate, but in the beginning, be as specific as possible. Which prospects would you welcome, and which would you want to steer clear from? If you have a large industry, which areas bore you or don't inspire as much joy as others? Be specific. Knowing these answers will help you create a strategy that will groom your business according to your vision.

What makes a brand more powerful is saying: We specialize in X, and in X alone. People may tell you to add on this service or that service so you can make side money to survive. But while add-on services may replenish the coffers once or twice, it really will just dilute your message, and send clients you don't really want.

2. Getting committed: Pick a Date

How can you commit yourself to a launch date? Almost eight months into our first pregnancy, I was extremely nervous, doubting my ability to be a good parent. I felt trapped and scared that I would fail. But regardless of whether I was ready, my son would still be born, and I would still become a parent. I had to fail forward and succeed no matter what.

How do you put that type of accountability on yourself, so you do follow through and stay committed to your business, regardless of perfection? Just as you may announce your pregnancy to friends and family through social media, calculate a finite amount of time to launch your business, and let people know the start-date of your business. Remind people the date is coming. While committing yourself might feel like too much pressure, it is crucial to this process.

Most business owners drop out when they don't commit, even if they have found their business direction. Ideas die here, never to be pursued again. A start-date commitment will help you reach another level of fulfillment and growth. I am here to tell you, there *is* another level.

I can only imagine all the skepticism generating through your body right now as I say that. All of your experience in life has gotten you to this point, and I'm here to tell you that you can go even higher than that. But you won't really know that until you get there.

My wife and I have been together since 2001. We basically grew up together since the beginnings of our "adult" lives, and we know everything about each other. I would always say how much in love I was with her and how I couldn't see myself loving another human being as much I loved her. Then my son came along. And immediately after, I looked at her and said, "Wow, I don't love you THAT much."

I had reached a whole other level of love when my son was born, which could never be described or realized by anything other than experience. No movie, book, or words could ever convince me that there *is* a higher level of love that can be reached. My son had to show me the possibilities. Don't you owe yourself the same possibilities with running your own business? Would that possibility be worth the attempt? This is all tied in with COMMITTING yourself to a launch date. I'm not saying for you to quit your job, and just run your business. Just commit to a start-date. That's all. This isn't an "all or nothing" process. You don't have to choose "either/or." You can still have both, if you want to.

3. Consistent Practice: Plan for the Long Game

The real secret to success in any business, no matter how saturated your industry, is consistency. Consistency will get you to succeed where others have failed. And the only way you stay consistent in your business is by making sure you stay in your joy.

As long as you enjoy what you're doing in your business, you will be able to withstand failure, disappointment, delayed successes, and act with the right perspective so that your "negative" business experiences are temporary. The joys you experience in your business will remind you WHY you're on this path to begin with and will give you the desire to persist. You will have something to look forward to, knowing you get to have fun in your job.

Another way to stay consistent is to enlist help from others to hold you accountable and provide you with perspective when needed. Recently, I watched an interview with Nastia Liukin, five-time Olympic medalist discussing her trials and emotions during her training. She talked about feeling down-and-out, wanting to quit gymnastics, and move on to something else. Nastia wanted to give up because she chose a path that was too hard.

Nastia credited her wise mom for holding her accountable to her commitments, saying it was okay to quit if Nastia wanted to. But her mom wouldn't let her quit until she went through rigorous practice and experience. Once she got that practice and experience, Nastia was allowed to evaluate whether gymnastics was right for her. Having won five Olympic medals, she obviously didn't quit.

Sometimes having someone hold you accountable is all you need to keep going. Knowing that someone knows and understands what you're going through is enough to stay the course.

When I realized how oversaturated the photography industry was, I got extremely nervous. I saw all the reasons why I couldn't succeed based on my lack of experience, lack of skills, and tons of competitors. My doubts passed as I realized that what I possessed was the experience of running businesses in the past. My goal, I concluded, was to keep consistent for two years. That would provide enough time for competitors who lacked my level of business experience to shut down. For the next two years, I focused on creating the right marketing and sales strategies, kept taking photos and learning, and developed my business. I also "hired" my friends and family to hold me accountable to my business goals. When I experienced the challenging days, I would go to them, vent my frustrations, receive assurance from them, and carry on with the business. Sure enough, two years had passed, and my theory was correct: I had an established business, and the people who I thought were my competition had moved on to something else.

Your inner game directly affects your outer results. Your job is to stay consistent in your business in a way that's easily sustainable for you, so that you're able to outlast your perceived competition and bring to fruition the idea you started with.

When It Gets Emotional

I have observed, and personally experienced, stunted emotional behavior during the key actions of commitment, focus, and consistency in this stage of business exploration. This kind of emotional behavior could spell doom for your potential business on the spot. This is where most people panic and never further pursue the business beyond the exploration phase.

There are two common emotional blocks at this stage. Observe your own process and see if they have come up:

Too good to be true

Exploring my new venture of helping parents start a business after photography, I helped numerous parents transform their business ideas into visions. They'd find the initial stages of joy in their proposed businesses, get excited, asking for guidance and strategies on launching their ventures... then digress and stop. Once they were given a glimpse of a compelling future, they'd return to the familiar. Some clients have told me this joy was "too good to be true," or that feeling that entrepreneurial joy "all the time" was unrealistic.

I would acknowledge that feeling completely fulfilled in your work might seem foreign. I would add, as an aside, that it won't be so rosy all the time. "Do you love being a parent all the time?" I would say to them. "When your two-year-old is screaming 'No!' over and over again in your face, or won't get in the car seat?"

Just like parenting, there are days you'll be in love with your business and days when you're, well, less smitten. The key parallel is: YOU DON'T GIVE THE KID BACK. You see the growth and the change, and your efforts are rewarded just enough that you keep moving along. Doing what brings you joy in business will always give the good days an edge over the bad days, if you can stay in the right attitude. It's not too good to be true!

Doubt Resurfaces

As this process of business exploration plays out, you can see yourself creating, running, and owning a business. Then, boom! The past creeps in. Immediately grand visions start to fade away, replaced by memories of past failures and disappointments. Then you look at the mountain to climb called ENTREPRENEURSHIP, and the towering barricades in your way. You digress and tell yourself the feat is too high to climb and you are not capable of reaching the top.

This self-doubt always finds a way to creep back into our lives at the most inopportune times. For instance, you have successfully taken action to creating a new business. You've committed yourself to finding your joy, and you've actually found some joy along the way, when your old pal, Self-Doubt, wants to pay you a visit again just when you told him to go on an extended vacation.

When you start feeling self-doubt, take a break. Just as you might feel frustrated when your baby won't stop crying, no matter what you do, sometimes a small break can reduce the impact on your emotions. Realize that you are fine, and that what you're feeling is normal. Acknowledge the emotion, and don't act.

Typically, we make poor decisions when we act from a lousy state. Give yourself permission to step back or even stop. But don't quit. Put yourself on "time out" until the self-doubt subsides or no longer has any effect on you, and continue onward.

If you find yourself experiencing either of these two emotional entanglements—Too Good to be True or Doubt Resurfaces—or other emotions that fall in line with fear and doubt, know that you're on the right track and should keep going once you've given yourself some self-care. What you're feeling is extremely common and doesn't pertain to just to you.

I still go through these emotions when I start something new. Once, my wife and I found out we were pregnant with our second son, some old emotions showed up to pay me a visit. I started to question if I was going to be a good father, if I was capable of raising a second child while starting a new business, whether THIS time, I should get a job, etc. Despite me already having a kid and growing a business, I STILL doubted my ability to do it again with a second child (because the saying must be true: "1 is 1, but 2 is 20.") Am I capable of handling, raising, and guiding two children, let alone one?! Sure enough, as these emotions pass, I regain my sanity and remind myself that everything will be fine.

The point is that everyone goes through these emotions at some point. Chances are, you might be going through them now because you've glimpsed what is new and possible. So, it's only natural for you to question your abilities, especially because this is the unknown.

So, you think, "Phew. I don't have those emotions right now, and I feel committed."

What about *excuses*? Ahhh, excuses, more wily ways for our ego to protect us from getting into hot water for dreaming too big. If you deal with the fear, and the excuses pop up, good! You are right on time!

Excuses Make an Encore

All the excuses that we explored at the start of the book will rush to the front lines now tenfold because you can actually see your dream business. How does it feel to hear them now?

I am putting my family in harm's way by taking great risks to start a business. Who will pay the rent? Feed the kids? Pay for the vet? The car? Insurance?

Other people are smarter, and had lessons on how to do this, in some conference in some city I never attended. These accomplished business owners never could have possibly gone through the indecision and questioning that I am going through. They just started a business and suddenly they had opt-ins, and sell-throughs, and lead magnets, and radio spots, and Facebook ads.

You can further identify the negative voice in your head.

Bookmark this page, and come back to it. You will need to hear what I'm going to tell you.

Yes, people are smarter. Yes, starting a business has risks. What does that have to do with you? Sure, others had a head start. So what? That has no bearing on your success. If anything, others paved the way for you to reference and model off of, to copy and repeat. In terms of risk, I will teach later in this chapter some of my methods in mitigating risk. Right now, the only risk you've taken is thinking, maybe a few phone calls, some research for an unobtrusive week, maybe two.

Regardless of whether you DID "catch the bug" yet or not, it doesn't hurt to keep exploring. You can always return to Chapter Four again and re-boot. For those of you who felt so focused, motivated, and euphoric you actually missed a meal: Congratulations! You've been infected with the entrepreneurial virus, and it can linger as long as the common cold with children under four in your house. For those of you who continued to feel intense fear and felt compelled to do anything else but build your business, you are three feet from gold. You've struck on something, and this is where most ideas die.

We will spend at least two-thirds of our lives working. Call me a dreamer, but I want to be as fulfilled as possible during that time. In fact, fulfillment is my main criterion in this life. I would rather suffer temporary fear than a lifetime lacking fulfillment. Whenever I start a new business, I feel like I'm searching for hidden treasure. I ask myself, "Where can I find treasure this time"? I start searching for clues based on the last treasure I found. I keep searching until I find some joy, regardless of my fear. Once I find that joy, I dig deeper to see if I can sustain that joy. If I do—eureka!—I have a new business.

Chapter 6

Foundation

"Having a compelling 'why'."

Did you just see a flash of bright light? It's your brilliance emerging. Creating a business is not an exact science. It is a series of action steps. If you understand all the information up to this point, you are ready to go to the next level for your business.

The psychology of a new business owner is built on laying the foundation of and understanding your "why," and discovering joy in what you do on a daily basis. Your "why" is your fuel of persistence, to push you through all the fear, doubt, and worry that comes from you internally (and externally). Having a compelling "why," fueled by your newfound joy, can create the momentum needed to continue past self-doubt.

Your "why" can steer you to answer three questions:

1. What is my product or service?

2. Who is the ideal customer for my product or service?

3. How can I make this ideal customer aware of my product or service?

The only reason you might feel blocked with your business at this time is that your "why" isn't big enough. If we became parents by choice, we already had this concept about what parenting was. Have you ever listened to someone who wasn't a parent talk about being a parent? They have this vision of being parents. That vision is where joy starts. It's almost in the naiveté that it'll all go our way because we never plan for what is going to go wrong in our joy. If you knew all the truths about how many times your kids would stay glued to their phones, or eat donuts to get through an oil change appointment, or how many times you'll tell your kids to eat food they've dropped on the floor, you'd probably consider not having kids, after all.

So, go to that joy with your business. Live in the "why" fantasy, and trust that like your kids, you too will be fine as you build a business just as they were, regardless of them licking the railing at the zoo or washing their hands a fourteenth time in an hour.

Imagine that your business is now your new child that comes into your life. But this time, you get to CHOOSE everything about your child, from personality, to whom they hang out with, and how they will succeed in life. You'd never be able to do this with your child (you can try, but many parents with teens know it's a futile exercise.) So starting a business is where you get to wield that control. With your redirected power of control, you can envision how you want to shape your "kid," and how you would like that "kid" to impact the world.

We build the foundation by "modeling." (I don't mean you take to the runway; my God, being a parent and running a business, we're lucky we even have underwear on.) I mean the process of looking for role models. Before my son Sebastian was born, I observed parents and their kids of various ages. I watched the kids' interactions, but more importantly, noted how the parents got the kids to be well-behaved. I took mental notes about what I liked and didn't like about what I saw. I observed how they spoke to their children, their body language, the tone of their voices, and the gestures they used. I mimicked what I learned with Sebastian once appropriate, and sure enough, he responded very similarly to what I had envisioned.

You will take the same action as you develop your business by using mentors and business owners you admire as models for learning what type of business you want to "raise." Watch what other business owners do and replicate their actions, so you can replicate their results. Learn from other businesses. Take note of what you find appealing about them as well as what you don't find appealing.

If I want a business that focuses on adding value, then I focus on companies that I believe are adding value. Just as children's behaviors are the reflections of their parents' upbringing (or lack thereof), businesses operate based on the guidance of the owner or CEO. Align yourself with business owners who share your beliefs of adding value. Learn how they approached raising their businesses.

If you're having a hard time finding businesses that share your vision of adding value, look at business models you *don't* agree with and identify those very characteristics you wish to avoid. I find that articulating what you *don't like* about a business is much easier to find and decipher. By understanding what you don't like, you will move yourself closer to finding what type of business you want to create.

One of the biggest challenges I had with network marketing companies was their high-pressure sales tactics. I would often find myself confronted by the sense of an ultimatum or by heavy sales tactics whenever I interacted with anyone from these businesses. I didn't enjoy or like that approach. It was only after I made that distinction that I decided to look elsewhere for business ideas and found better business models that fit my vision and approach.

I know a parent, Joann, who shared a story with me about how she got into her business. Joann was approached by one of her friends to join her network marketing company, selling a specific makeup brand. Her friend did her "sales pitch," focusing on how wealthy Joann could become by getting into this business. She showed the bank statements of her managers, indicating all the passive income they got, and tried to sell Joann on a "wealthy" future with this product. Because the vision didn't align with Joann's, and she respectfully declined.

Years later, Joann was approached by another friend selling the same product using the same business model of networking marketing. However, this time was different. This other friend focused more on the product, how convenient and functional the product was, and how easy the product was to sell. Joann was immediately hooked. She saw all the benefits of the product and knew she could sell it because the product added value. Joann signed up right away.

As you dive into business, many of your morals and values will play a part in what type of business you will create and "raise." The saying holds true: Birds of a feather flock together. During this time, meeting business owners, you will get a sense of what strategies speak to you and what strategies repel you. Talk to those "parents" of businesses you found so well-behaved and ask them how they were so discerning and resourceful. Then start approaching your business as you would your parenting. Over time, you will have a sense of your business's character, and how to raise your business according to your personal vision.

Your Ultimate Resource

I would be doing you an injustice if I didn't tell you that your ultimate resource is YOU. If you're able to use this resource, your success will know no boundaries. You will get to experience new realities, and live your dreams. All you have to do is use this resource.

The Parenting You

From one parent to another, I'm informing you that you have gobs of experience to start a business because of your ability to navigate the waters of pint-sized Neanderthals and insolent teens. Building a business is hardly scary when you put into perspective becoming a first-time parent.

Can you remember when you found out that you were going to be a first-time parent? I'm going to gamble on the fact that after the initial shock of pregnancy, you thought, I have no idea what I am doing.

As the pregnancy moved along, you read a multitude of parenting books and thought, "I got this." You made charts and plans. You bought all the right products. Then when your child came into this world, you were sidelined by unexpected scenarios, demands, all of which caused you to let some of your rules slip.

During my wife's pregnancy, we talked about the great parents we would be: We would never let our boy watch TV all day, never give him a phone during dinner, never let him eat food that had fallen on the ground, never let him touch his food without cleaning his hands, and never get mad at him. Today, I'm happy to report that we broke ALL those rules and with our second child, NEVER made those rules. We're still great parents!

Business is no different. There are times in business when your plans don't succeed, when something doesn't go your way, or you don't achieve what you initially planned on. Have you ever said yes to a project that you knew wasn't a good fit because you needed the money, or saying things like, "I'm never going to let my business life affect my personal life," "I will never answer the phone after 6 p.m.," "I won't never work on the laptop in bed," "I won't ever answer emails at 2 a.m.," and "I will never put business before family"? Like the saying goes, "Goal are set in stone. Plans are set in sand." As a parent, you have two key characteristics that are vital for creating a business: resilience and flexibility. You can adapt and change quickly when your best laid plans dive-bomb.

GO, Ready, Set!

Starting a business as a parent is not just about the action steps. Action steps about the ins and outs of a business are inherently very simple. We all know we need business cards, a website, a logo, a marketing plan, a business plan, funding, manufacturing, headshots, video production, slogan, guiding principles. WARNING: This is STILL not the time to focus on the "marketing minutiae" of business. These are the minor details of a business that don't actually make a business. Please stay away from these details as long as possible (as I speak from experience). I promise I will let you know when this time comes, but here is why I give you this cautionary tale.

Even if you drift into fancy website fantasyland for half a day, what truly prevents parents from starting and succeeding in a business is the weak mindset they possess before going into the business. Without the proper foundation of a strong mindset, you will be vulnerable to events and circumstances that stop your business, possibly even before the business begins.

As parents without a clear vision of what you want out of your parenting experience, you will always be in a state of reaction. If your kids are mad, and you let them get you mad, your reaction is coming from a state of powerlessness and from doing something you don't want to do. You will also become vulnerable to people's opinions. The same applies in business.

In *The Outliers,* Malcolm Gladwell posits a concept called the Law of 10,000 Hours. He suggests that, in order to achieve "expert level" status in any field, you have to possess at least 10,000 hours of deliberate practice. The psychology of "Parenting a Business" argues that your 10,000 hours of business experience comes from the countless hours being a parent. You've already achieved "expert" status for a business but need to connect the two together. If you have your business mindset locked in sync with your parenting identity, I'm confident you will be able to create a business you'll be proud of.

How Your First "No" Can Build Confidence

Making your first sale slowly chips away at any doubts you have over whether you should be starting a business. Feeling nervous, unprepared, or hesitant because your product or service is "not ready" is normal. Yet it's also such a powerful feeling that it often prevents parents from launching their business. If you put too much pressure on "getting it right" the first time, you will fail to launch. All attention and focus go into getting a "yes" and on preventing a prospect from saying "no." If you get a "no," or several "no's," in the beginning, you may assume your business is not worthy, and all the fears and excuses will come rushing back to keep you from continuing.

Here is some advice I was given a while back that made me fearless in the selling stages of my business: If ever there was a time to fail, NOW is the time. Most first-time business owners focus on trying to do everything right in the first few months because they don't want to screw up or miss out on a sale. Everything feels so tenuous and fragile, like a newborn baby. A better focus is to market and sell ... and adjust accordingly.

Right now, you have no experience selling your product or service. You don't know how you sell or how your business will be received in the marketplace. This is your time to learn about your processes and experience how to actually sell your product or service.

The reason why NOW is the time to fail is because your company is small, and you can build confidence. You may be afraid of failing until you fail, and then trust me, you realize it's not that bad. I've done it, I know! Once you no longer have the fear of failure, anything is possible, and you are willing to take more risks. You become Elon Musk!

The same applies to the first family vacation with little kids. Especially road trips. Based on previous road trips, parents quickly learn what to load up the car with and what kinds of activities will keep the kids occupied. You don't stay at home for the rest of your kids' lives just because one road trip went awry, do you? No, you learn what worked in the past and what didn't.

No one knows anything about your business yet. If you're small and you fail, your failure will have very little impact. No one knows you exist, so your "failures" may not cause a ripple in the marketplace. It's when you're a bigger business, with lots of clients and followers, that you can less afford to fail. When your company is known and your business moves are followed and shared by a community of loyal customers, that's when failure must be minimized, when your actions must be completely thought out and calculated. When you get to a certain a point, part of your business planning will deal with managing things when they go wrong. Don't panic. We aren't there yet. But I can assure you, through the actionable steps in this book, by the time you get there, you won't be as worried about failing because you'll have your contingencies mapped out.

The Repetition of Car Trips or Preparing the Diaper Bag

During your initial selling process, maintaining an objective outlook will keep you focused on building a business that you envision. In fact, let's step back and simplify what a business really is. A business is nothing more than a collection of systems. A collection of systems is a step-by-step process in which you will develop a better idea of what to focus on when you start selling your product or service.

In parenting a business, your initial questions will reveal the simplest components of your proposed business. A business system can be broken down to three core components:

- Create a product and service.

- Sell the product and service.

- Fulfill the order.

All the rest is noise!

You will repeat these three steps over and over again to increase your chances of predicting the outcome of your actions. Repetition is the key to creating a predictable outcome.

I'd like to share a parenting experience that might help articulate this process of repetition for predictability. About four weeks after our first son was born, my wife and I attempted to go out to a family gathering for the first time. We were so excited and nervous at the same time. We anticipated that this process of *leaving the house*, which normally took us 20 minutes to do, would probably take us 45 minutes with a newborn. What an optimistic calculation!

We got ready in our predicted 20 minutes. Then my son started to cry because he was hungry. So my wife feeds him while I watch TV. Now my son is fed, and the car is packed.

SUCCESS, we're out in 45 minutes … until … my son decides to spit up all over his outfit. Great. Let's change him. After changing him, he decides to poop. Awesome! So we change his diaper. As we're readying to leave, I forget to pack the diaper bag. Okay, time to pack diapers, wipes, extra clothes, blankets in case Sebastian got cold, and the lifesaving "shhh-ing" noise-maker, in case he cried in the car. Bag is packed, and we're ready to go.

We get in the car, and my wife asks, "Did you also pack the stroller?"

CRAP! I go back in the house for the stroller. Once the stroller is in the car, we're ready to, until my son decides to fuss around and poops again. *AHHH!* We're never going to leave! We get out of the car, change his diaper, and attempt to leave one more time. By that point, what was projected to take 45 minutes ended up taking an hour and a half! Also, my wife and I are so exhausted from just trying to get out of the house that we didn't even feel like going to the party anymore.

Fortunately, my wife is a forward-thinker. Learning from this experience that so much time could have been saved if we had just been a little bit more prepared, she packs the diaper bag with all the essentials ahead of time before we go out again. She also instructs me to stop watching TV as she's nursing and, instead, pack the car so she doesn't have to wait. From those decisions alone, we shaved 30 minutes off our time getting out of the house the next time.

She took this process one step further. On our changing table, she created compartments and organized all the diapers, wipes, ointments, and changing clothes so that they were within arm's reach, and we weren't fumbling around for items during a speedy diaper change. With enough adjustments to our system and with enough repetition, we successfully got our process down to less than 30 minutes. *Audience applause*

I hope by now you're starting to see that all your parenting experiences from functioning on no sleep to creating simpler ways for leaving the house with a toddler are skills that transfer rather effortlessly into the makings of a business. Your next steps are to channel those skills into your business to create a predictable outcome.

Chapter 7

The Business Starts to Grow Up

*"A yes or no isn't as important as knowing
why you're getting a yes or no."*

It's astonishing to me that "parenting" isn't a course taught in business schools. Parenting involves many of the most vital skill sets you need to also succeed in business. Every business owner (who is a parent) I've brought up these similarities with would invariably laugh at how true this statement is. Being on both sides of the spectrum, they all see what I see: Parents have the edge to being great business owners. If that's true, how do we, as parents, harness this edge to creating a successful business?

You have learned about creating your product and service. Now we need to market/sell and then fulfill the order. Sounds simple, and it can be, without over-complication. My desire is for you to see how your life experiences have groomed you to create and run your own business.

You created the products and services from your weekly hours of exploration. You built a psychological foundation for your business, keeping in mind the pitfalls and how, in a pinch, you can solve a problem by applying your own parenting resourcefulness. You have also considered making your first sale. That means you are (gasp!) moving into officially marketing and selling your products and services in your business.

When selling your product for the first time (or tenth time), your focus is on how best to sell the product and how effective to make your process. As I mentioned in the previous chapter, getting a "yes" or "no" is not crucial for your business right now.

What's important is knowing *why* you're getting a "yes or no." Knowing what did work and didn't work will create the information you need to develop your most effective marketing system. And that system, in turn, will eventually yield predictable outcomes for your business, i.e., more sales.

As a business owner, your job is to market and sell your product and service with the focus of creating a predictable outcome. When you're selling your product or service, notice how you sell and how effective your strategy is. Evaluate what works well and doesn't seem to work well. Get feedback on your approach, and don't be afraid to ask for feedback. More than likely, your customers are willing to give you their opinion. Use that information to make your processes better. So again, now is not the time to get your selling perfect. Now is the time to learn about your business, while developing your business as the same time.

Talking to your kids and getting feedback from them and listening is the best comparison. Get into a dialogue when their child is upset. You adjust your approach based on your child's feedback. Your kid doesn't respond well to being yelled at, but your kids do very well with bribes and candy. Adjust your clients' needs based on what they want versus what you think they want.

Seven Key Parenting Traits to Market and Sell Your Products or Services

I devised seven fundamental traits of parents that, when applied smartly, are surefire ways to run a successful business.

1. Product/Service Testing or "Keep Trying New Things Until They're Happy and Quiet"

A business is fundamentally launched with the creation of an idea for a product or service. You envision that your product or service will be well-received by the public, and how great you will feel with their praise. This is all well and good for your self-confidence, but, before any of that, you need to be certain that what you have to offer is what the public actually wants. Product- and service-based businesses fail all the time. That in mind, ask yourself what will make yours succeed where others have failed? One strategy that might offer some certainty in the beginning is product/service (PS) testing. As parents, we call this "Keep trying new things until they're happy and quiet".

PS testing is extremely important when developing your product/service for your business. PS testing is researching what your target market wants, values, desires, and needs based on your business. Before you jump off the deep end of a pool thinking you'll learn to swim when you hit the water, you test the waters with very little risk. Your PS testing is a showcase of your business value to a small group of people that consists of your ideal target market, and receiving feedback from them. You probe for clues as to what they focus on and what they don't even notice. You see what is important to them and what may not be much of a factor at all. This research is vital to how you develop and market your business in the future.

In parenting, this process comes in many forms. When my first son was born, my wife and I were "prepared" with all the toys, gadgets, and widgets that would help his development. We organized all the furniture for seamless transitions from holding to changing his diapers to putting him in the rocker. After he was born, everything we had setup worked like a charm ... except for one item—the rocker.

We found out very quickly how opinionated a newborn could be. He immediately showed his displeasure of the rocker we had purchased, crying every second he was in it. "How could this be?" we thought. The reviews on Amazon were amazing! So we replaced that rocker with one that rocked back and forth versus side to side. We tried a third rocker, this one more elevated. Nope. More crying. With the fourth rocker, we felt like he digressed; now he cried *after* we took him out of the rocker. By the fifth rocker, we were praying for some semblance of hope that he would like ANYTHING. And to our surprise, he stopped crying. YES! We succeeded by adding data based on what he wanted—just as you would with a consumer of your product. Your consumer won't cry their way through their opinions (at least you hope not), but they will vocalize unspecific dissatisfaction that you'll need to analyze, adjust, and come back with new options.

You won't necessarily need five tries. Welcome to the A/B process. Do you like blue or green? How about green or purple? Provide target markets with simple questions. If you are debating a logo design, ask which one do you like the best and why. You learn quickly how what you assumed your customers wanted may not be the case at all.

In other words, the rocker you choose may have all the best "ratings" from other users, but that doesn't mean that YOUR child will rate it the same way. Only by going through the motions, taking the time to learn their preferences will you be able to truly KNOW and act accordingly.

Here is a second example. As my son grew, my wife and I noticed what a picky eater he was. I will concede that we were extremely protective of what he ate when he started on solid foods. That behavior might have created a child who doesn't like certain textures of food and won't eat anything he doesn't like.

When he started preschool, my wife had the hardest time trying to figure out what to feed him. She bought different types of foods and snacks of different brands, shapes and sizes. Sometimes he ate his food, sometimes not. We kept trying new foods until he started showing us what he gravitated towards. Once we learned what he liked, we started to adjust our grocery shopping habits to make sure we got foods he would eat.

Whether you have a "picky eater" on your hands or an infant that needs to have a certain type of rocker to sleep on, the lessons for your business are clear.

In your business, when developing your product or service, research your customers and what they want in the same way as you'd "research" your child's needs/wants. Acquiring this information is vital to how you create your product/service, and how you will market and sell as well.

2. Persistence > No

Once you have your product/service developed, your next step is to figure out ways to market and sell. Selling and negotiation tends to be such a hard task for most people. They fear they will be too pushy, rejected, or fail. Every parent has or will become master negotiators through interacting with their children. Some of our most challenging conflicts with our children have prepared us for these sales fears. We have all experienced our children throwing the awful, seemingly never-ending temper tantrum. They cry, scream, yell, thrash, and their favorite word seems to be, "No!" At times like this, they are beyond reason or consolation. No amount of consoling, promises of ice cream can break their spell. In business, we call that an "irate" customer.

Children have an uncanny quality of persistence when they want something. They are the best salesmen, embodying the idea that a "no" means a definite "maybe." Whenever my son wants something, like some chocolate chip cookies, he'll first come up to me and politely ask for some. Knowing that he hasn't eaten lunch yet, I'll tell him that he needs to wait until after he has lunch. He agrees and walks away. A minute later he comes back and politely again asks for some cookies, to which I have the same response. History repeats itself about 15 times in 15 minutes to the point where my resolve has crumbled, and my desires to not want to spoil his appetite are all but vanished. I cave in and give him the cookies, so I can go back to whatever I was doing 15 minutes ago.

When selling your product, embody your children's persistence, not taking rejection personally and persisting until you get the outcome you desire. There may be times when you might have to adjust your tactics, but the important component to your negotiations is your outcome.

3. Rejection Resilience

I don't know about you, but I've taken more rejection from my two-year-old in a month than I have in any business I've ever created. Every time I offer to help him, he wants his mom. Every other time he asks for me, I go to him, and he pushes me away. I admit I took his rejections pretty personally in the beginning. But as time went on, I started to develop a tolerance for his rejection, stopped taking his actions personally and accepted his behavior as part of the process of parenting.

In business, if you jump all-in, you will experience massive rejection. Rejection does not equate to failure, but point to signs that you need to make adjustments in your approach. Rejection in business is part of the process. If you can approach your business (and rejection) the same way you approach addressing your kids, selling won't have to be so hard and intimidating. You're already groomed for selling because you have been rejected by your own offspring. If you can learn to disassociate yourself from rejection as personal, who cares about being rejected by strangers? The point is that your kids have already given you the experience of the "negative" aspects of selling, so you're ready!

4. Can a two-year-old relate?

Since I am a serial entrepreneur, I make a daily habit of consuming the advertisements, magazines, billboards, posters, and other marketing collateral that's everywhere in our society. I observe the overall message and presentation, and then I look at the imagery, content, and positioning to evaluate whether I think that particular marketing piece hit the mark with what I'm assuming to be its target audience. I'm not always right or wrong, but staying connected to how others approach their marketing helps me to understand perspective when creating my own marketing. Some of the worst collateral I've seen came from advertisements with big fancy words that confused the consumer as to what the product actually did. The words were unnecessary and ineffective in promoting the service-based company's brand and the impression the company was trying to make, to the point where you have no idea what the company actually does. I call this Overcompensating Marketing.

We optimize our efficiency using data metrics to quantify the effectiveness of the subject. You're left wondering, "What do you do exactly with your company?"

The opposite of Overcompensating Marketing is Simplification Marketing. A company uses buzz words like "innovation," the most common buzzword in marketing (so much so that word itself is no longer innovative).

My conclusion was that whoever came up with those advertisements were using terms that they normally used on a regular basis, but that their customers may not know what they necessarily meant.

I have adopted a philosophy about marketing that has worked time and time again. It's overly simplistic, yet universally effective: Less is more. When I talk to businesses about their marketing message, I ask them to articulate their business so a two-year-old can understand. What do you do? When someone buys a house for the first time, do they know what escrow is? Surprisingly, many have a hard time with this exercise. If you can't explain your business to a two-year-old, then you have overcomplicated your business. And if a two-year-old won't be able to understand your business, you might be mistaken in assuming that an adult will understand your explanations.

Just keep it simple. If you sell life insurance, then sell it. Don't tell me that you maximize life expectancy with funding from the global markets.

5. What Did You Say?

I made this mistake in my photography business. Normally, a bid would be requested on a photography project, whether it was a wedding or a company marketing campaign. The prospect then wants to know what kind of camera I use. It was an odd question, but I assumed that since they asked, they understood photography terminology. I would tell them my camera model, the highest ISO settings with no noise, the aperture ranges, and the megapixel count. Looking at their reactions, I might as well have been talking gibberish. None of the terms I used were anything they'd ever heard of before or had any reference to. I realized that they didn't actually care about my camera's features but were looking for someone with an expertise to do a solid job.

I understood then that I needed to approach all clients as if they knew nothing about photography, and I used concepts they could understand. I would start with really basic explanations of the camera. As parents, you learn this skill when your kid has his own language that only you understand. With my son, because of his repetition, my wife and I heard exactly what he said without question. Other people would visit us, though, and have a hard time understanding what he was saying. I became his translator, so others could respond accordingly.

Be careful about using terminology that people might not understand. Learn to develop a language specifically for your customers, speaking on their level. Even if the words you use are common terms in your industry, always be mindful of who you're speaking to and of the likelihood that they'll understand what you are saying. You don't want your selling process get lost in translation, where you may lose out on a sale because you weren't speaking in clear, easy-to-understand terms.

Once you've successfully generated sales, the transaction isn't finished. If anything, the transaction has just begun. This is where companies that are destined to fail actually do fail. They may have figured out how to market and sell effectively, but fall short in delivering a quality product or service experience to their customers. This last component of your business is vital to its sustainable growth, in reputation, repeat customers, and referrals.

Once you've successfully generated a sale through our marketing and sales strategies, you need to make sure that your fulfillment process is just as effective.

6. Set the Standard

When fulfilling an order on your product/service, be mindful of the expectations that your customer has about how you'll deliver on your value. The more involved and knowledgeable your customers are about the transaction process, the more comfortable they'll feel about your business.

You might inform them of the date or date range of when their order will be fulfilled, along with any variables they might anticipate, and the standard of the goods or services purchased. By setting the standard, you control their expectations, and thus, you control the quality of the experience. How you deliver on your product or service might be as important as the product or service itself. The conclusion of the transaction is part of the "experience" your customers have in your business, and needs to be considered carefully.

As a parent, I have made some errors in my delivery of my promises to my son, and he made sure I knew my mistakes. Remember the cookies my son asked for? Well, we had these large cookies that I thought were too big for him to eat. I thought they'd crumble on the floor after he took a bite. So logically, I broke the cookie in half. That way, he could eat half at a time and minimize any spills. The moment that cookie split in half, his world was torn apart. His eyes widened with tears. He let out a scream that could be heard from Mars and started to cry uncontrollably. As he cried, my wife came into the kitchen, shaking her head.

"Did you break the cookie in half? He likes to receive his cookies whole as a circle."

And sure enough, as my son cries, he shouts, "Circle, circle. Baby wants circle."

Yes, this IS a true story. And YES, I break his cookies in half before I give him any. After my wife explained why he was upset, I let our son know ahead of time that I will break the cookies and explained why. Remarkably, my explanation was well received, and he no longer throws a tantrum when he gets halves.

As kids have their expectations for how life should be, don't be surprised if customers and clients have similarly preconceived expectations. You must control your transaction by articulating ahead of time what the client should expect on delivery of your goods or services.

7. Check in Time

At the end of your product or service sales transaction, you have the opportunity to learn from your clients by asking for feedback. You value their opinion; it will help your business grow, and therefore, it is crucial to take the time to learn about what they experienced. Their feedback means you now have information that you can use to make your business better, from product/service development to customer engagement to goods and services delivery.

As my son gets older and experiences new events, I constantly check in with him to see how he's doing, and how he's feeling. From preschool to being a big brother, I can imagine how overwhelmed he must feel about all the changes he is going through. Being a big brother (at two years old), I see him adjusting and learning how to evolve to the times. He helps out when his brother cries. But he can also act out to get attention from his parents. He loves when we spend time with just him and loves his alone time too. I've always felt that checking in with him and being in touch with how he's doing makes my decisions as a parent clearer to make.

As a business owner, you must always be in touch with your customers/clients. Understand their needs, wants, and desires. Understand their fears and stresses. See if there are ways you can alleviate those fears in your business. Constantly check in with them and make sure you do everything you can to meet their needs (sometimes through the eyes of a parent), and your business will never go hungry.

The Secret Component: Self Care

As with the parenting life, the business life will have its moments of stress-filled days, sleepless nights, long hours, and no breaks. You may question your abilities and doubt your resolve to keep going. You may want to crawl into bed, turn off your phone, and never think about business again. It's in these moments where you'll most need the final component in your business for long-term success. You must create the system of *self-care*. Whether you're a business owner or a parent or both, "bad days" are inevitable. How you get through these moments in business can be mirrored in the strategies you've developed as a parent.

When my son was born, I had a tough time adjusting to the lack of sleep and the countless hours of crying. Compounded over time, I developed some not-so-ideal frustrations that I'm sure my son could feel. Those emotions manifested themselves in such a way that my son didn't want me to help him with anything and only have his mom help him. With no sleep and lots of frustration inside of me, I concluded that my son was holding a grudge against me and wondered how long that grudge would last. I vented my frustrations to a friend. She laughed and said, "Jeremy, babies that age don't hold grudges. They just respond to energy, just like you or me, but on a pure reaction level. He's just reacting to your negative emotions right now."

After her talk, I quickly told my wife that I needed to take a break. I went out for a drive by myself, ate some food, worked out, and let go of my tension. I went to beach, watched the sunset, and embodied the idea that my son was showing me how much I needed to work on grounding myself again. I came back refreshed, and ready to try again. The moment I walked in the door, guess who wanted me to hold him? My beautiful teacher, who also happens to my son. Thank you for the lesson.

As business owners, we may experience events that we don't plan for or don't want, yet we have to keep going. Although our customers may not be as forward as kids are in reaction to our off-kilter energy, they most certainly can sense the tension. Their reactions may be subtle, such as postponing a meeting or delaying a transaction for a later date. When these events occur, check in with yourself, and make sure to apply self-care when needed. You deserve to take breaks when needed.

Disconnect from Bad Days

Before I was a parent, I would observe in awe how parents would be so patient with their child, who'd be screaming and shouting at them in public. They would just sit and be present with their screaming toddler, smile and say, "Yeah ... he's just having a bad day."

I never understood how such compassion could be so genuine for parents, and I questioned whether I could have a similar response with my own kids. As I've grown as a parent, what I've learned is that "bad days" are very common in the toddler stage of a child's development. Maybe I'm just blessed with a very "in-tuned" child, but I've lost track of how many tantrums he has in a week and have also adopted the mindset of him just having a "bad day." The cool part is seeing how other parents can understand and relate when your kid acts up, and you just add that up to him having a "bad day." There is this immediate disconnect from any expectation of how my child *should* behave on such occasions.

In your business, when events don't go your way, learn to disconnect, and mark that up to a "bad day," and move on. If your business is throwing a tantrum and isn't doing what you planned, say that your business is having a "bad day," and you'll try again tomorrow.

Now that you have an idea of what to expect in all three phases, it's time to commit to your business, knowing how to take care of yourself along the way. You can return to this chapter or any of the previous chapters at any time as part of your road map.

With your first sales come the energy to keep going. Use this momentum and commit to yourself, following the steps to Parenting a Business.

I'm ready when you are!

Chapter 8

Don't Stop Moving

"Throw spaghetti on the wall, and see what sticks!"

There is no delicate way to put this, but in order to be successful, you'll never stop planning for your business. Just like with raising kids and adapting to their different ages and needs, you will plan and strategize in a business—constantly. After you launch, your goal is to offer your valuable and original services to the world in a continuous way. Believe me, I know about those days when you want to throw in the towel on parenting. "Screw it," you want to tell them, "watch YouTube all day. Mommy and Daddy need a nap." With your business, you'll have those moments too, but you don't stop being a business owner, just like you don't stop parenting.

If there is any area I have outlined in the previous chapters that you feel you neglected or dialed in when creating your business, that's okay for now. We can examine places we avoid like the plague in our businesses at a later juncture, and even consider hiring others to help us. Now is the time to get excited. Nervous? Likely. Ready?! ABSOLUTELY … not. Starting your business will always involve mixed emotions. On one hand, you're excited to start something new, creating a business based on *your* vision. On the other hand, you're putting yourself out there, not knowing whether your vision will be well-received and accepted as valuable. So much uncertainty can cause someone to turn back and not launch.

The good news is that that person will not be you! You've gone through the steps of finding your joy, addressing your fears, and distinguishing your brand from others. And most importantly, you are a PARENT. You are ready to launch your business!

What Now?

Even when you get your first sale, you never want to let up on the accelerator and fall back on your laurels. You need to plan more than ever to continuously grow your business. Your focus now is on exposure, making your company visible.

Exposure is all about leverage. What can you leverage to expose your brand to a bigger audience? Social media, networking events, asking your personal network for their contacts, purchasing leads, or putting an ad out in a circulated magazine or newspaper? You might ask someone with a big network to endorse you by giving them your product and service. Continuously marketing your business when you launch ensures your business will have a life. I have met countless business owners who have great value to offer and close down because they fail to put themselves out there properly. They turn into another entry in that big volume entitled, *Great Ideas that No One Knows About.*

My son is a persistent marketer. He always captures my attention no matter what. One morning, I was watching a football game. My son runs up to me, looking for attention. He gets in between me and the TV and says, "Good morning, Dad." I say hello and continue watching football. He then sits down next to me and starts tapping me on the hand until I acknowledge him. I look over, and he gives me this innocent, cheesy smile.

"Good morning, Dad," he repeats, in a sweet and charming voice.,

"Good morning," I reply, and go back to watching football. Finally, he stands up on the couch, puts both hands on my face and turns my head to look at him.

"Good morning Dad," he says with a smile.

I finally turn off the TV.

"Good morning. Is there something you'd like me to do?"

His smile grows bigger as he proclaims, "No TV. Let's play".

Well played, son. Well played.

I'm not suggesting that you should grab your customers by

the face to get their attention. Rather, I'm saying don't be afraid to try creative strategies to market your business, and be relentless to get a result.

There's a Bill Gates quote that I use all the time: "Throw spaghetti on the wall and see what sticks." In other words, your goal is to try everything you can to gain exposure and see what works. You don't have to necessarily be elegant in your approach. Just be effective. As I instructed in chapter six, you can refer to your research of other businesses in your industry that provide a similar product/service that you do, and see how they market. Look at your "role models" in business and understand their strategies. What can you make that's uniquely yours with your personality in your business? Don't limit yourself to what your industry has done, and think that's all you can do. Be creative and use your imagination as if you were your two-year-old child.

Try several strategies and evaluate continuously how effective they are with potential consumers. If you are mindful in your approach to marketing, you set yourself up to win. If you buy into a marketing strategy, try it. See how it works. If you think you can make the strategy better, try that, and gauge your results. Have the courage to experiment with your marketing approach, even if you think the results may not be favorable. The goal isn't to be right 100% of the time. The goal is to learn about which marketing strategies work and which don't. Creativity may serve you well, but don't discount the value of tried-and-true marketing systems. There is a reason they work.

If you happen to find an effective marketing strategy for your business, celebrate! Caveat, however: Don't depend on having that one strategy work every time. Diversify your approach, and have multiple ways of generating leads, knowing you don't need to depend on big marketing dollars to start. Set yourself up to win by not putting too much pressure on any single strategy working. Instead of one marketing strategy working 100% of the time, try having five marketing strategies working 20% of the time. That way, if one strategy doesn't perform in a given month, you have four others to fall back on and generate leads.

In the early days of my photography business, I didn't have many marketing strategies to tap into. I had very little experience and exposure. So, I began my marketing efforts in live networking groups. I joined a weekly networking meeting that helped me gain the exposure and experience I needed. I was only marketing this one way, and then the leads slowed down. Next, I turned to social media. Now, along with my networking, I created profiles on several review-based websites and asked customers for their positive feedback on my services. Soon, I had three websites generating leads for me. Finally, with all the closed business I received from all my marketing, I began to receive referrals from past clients. Today, I monitor every avenue of marketing I have in place, and make sure I'm maximizing my exposure from these strategies. I'm not implying that they're all successful all the time, but when one marketing strategy doesn't do well in a given month, I can rely on the others to pick up some the slack.

You may feel overwhelmed or lost when you start your marketing. That's very normal. Don't worry about failure. The only real failure is if you do nothing yet have a great product or service that no one knows about. The key is to keep trying new ways to grab your target market's attention, assess the results, and pivot accordingly.

As my son is getting older, I'm noticing how he is starting to ignore me when I talk to him or call his name. I'll tell him to eat dinner, and he'll continue playing with his toys as if he didn't hear me. After a while, I was getting frustrated that he wouldn't respond to me when I spoke to him. Rather than getting mad and raising my voice, I decided to have some fun with him and see if I'm any good at marketing. I figured if I could grab my son's attention, I could get ANYONE's attention.

I started with saying his name over and over again, the way he did with me. No success. "Okay," I thought, "let's try calling him from a different room in a loud, stern tone to see if he will respond to that." He doesn't even look in my direction. Fine. Let's play his favorite songs on my phone and start dancing. SUCCESS! He runs into the dining room and starts dancing with me. I immediately turn off the music and tell him "Time for dinner!"

Marketing your business can be as straightforward or as creative as you'd like. Reflect on ways you get your children's attention, and I'm sure you'll find how creative you really are, then apply the same creativity to marketing. Make this exercise fun. Your children will probably be your best customer-guinea pigs, because they're very familiar with you, and they'll be tougher to market to—especially since they already know how to tune you out.

Approach your business education like your education in parenting. We were all first-time parents once. In preparation, we read blogs, talked to parents we know, read the big parenting books, and watched videos on parenting. Once you become a parent, all that knowledge you collected gets transferred into actionable steps. The feedback from those steps tells you whether you like or don't like how you're evolving as a parent. Soon, you discover how you want to proceed, based on feedback, and find strategies based on your real-life experiences and distinctions.

It is the exact same with launching and marketing your business. You can follow the "recipes" that others have created, but don't be afraid to alter and adjust depending on what works for you and your business.

Absolutely Not ... Means Yes

Launching your business can be an exciting time, but also a stressful time. If you are fortunate to have a supporting community of friends and family, you have a head start on creating your marketing and sales strategies. They may buy your products (or hire you for your services). They may refer their networks to you, knowing you were once there for them. When this happens, accept the offer; do not turn down their business or referrals.

After launching my photography business, my skill level wasn't anywhere near what I wanted, but I knew I could still add value and learn along the way. I kept taking photos in my spare time and shared them on social media. My first "big job" came from a friend of mine who asked if I photographed weddings. Without hesitation, I said, "Absolutely not," and told him I could refer him to very experienced wedding photographers. Knowing I was the right man for the job, he smiled, and told me they weren't looking for a big wedding photographer, but someone to capture moments for their dinner banquet. I still pushed back, but knew I had to step out of my comfort zone at some point, and take on a project that had pressure and importance. You can redo a headshot, but you can't retake a candid wedding photo. Looking back now, this opportunity was the best experience for pushing me to the next level.

Before the "big day," I asked friends if I could borrow their lenses (which were more advanced than my equipment at the time), practiced taking photos, scouted the venue days before to get a better idea of what I was getting into, and tried to cover every variable I could so as not to screw up this big event.

The day of the wedding, I was extremely nervous and hoped I did a good job for them. I didn't want to ruin their big day by giving them poor quality images. Once I got to the venue, I started taking photos of family members who were already there. After taking some photos, the couple arrived, and my anxiety shot through the roof. The couple, happy as could be, welcomed me with open arms. I thanked them for the opportunity to photograph them on their big day and told them how much I wanted to do a great job for them.

"We're so happy you could help us. Our cousin speaks so highly of you, and *we* are so grateful to have you," they both said, beaming about their big day.

From that moment, I was ON because of my friend's confidence in me. When someone who believes in you, gives you one of your first breaks, puts your faith in you, and no stock in your fear. Faith will help you focus on the client and the product or service they bought. Through pushing away the fear, your special talents will be quickly revealed.

We made our way to the courtyard in the hotel, and I observed their demeanor shift. They grew very uncomfortable and awkward, and the bubbly couple that had just greeted me became shy. My anxiety disappeared as I saw my focus was on making them comfortable again.

I told jokes to relax them and coached them on certain poses that would make the photos livelier and more vibrant. I would "model" postures and showed them exactly how they should pose together. With this approach, the couple immediately transformed back to the original couple I had met. Once I helped them let down their guard, I was able to capture how fun this couple was and their deep love for each other. The photos really took care of themselves.

Once the banquet started, I captured all the moments that were special to the couple, from speeches to dances. The family kept interacting with me, encouraging me to engage in the festivities with them. Again, the photos took care of themselves. At the end of the night, we left smiling, and hugging goodbye. I felt a part of the family.

A few days later, my friend calls me and says, "Jeremy, my cousin and family LOVE you. They were so happy that you photographed their wedding."

I thanked him again for the opportunity and told him how amazing his family was. I couldn't express the enormity of my gratitude to have such a fun business experience and knew I wanted to feel that way on every job. You can have fun doing what you love. It validated the statement, do what you love, and the money will come.

Today, if I were to look at the photos I took at that wedding, I could tell you how I would change my approach, and what I did technically "wrong." None of that matters because what this experience taught me most is my "value" to my customers. It was more about the "experience" I gave them, not the photos. I made the couple feel extremely relaxed during their photo session, and they loved the results. I discovered my magic in this business was my ability to connect with others and get them to relax in front of a camera.

Once I realized my unique sales angle as a photographer, I adapted my marketing with an emphasis on human connection. That message is what makes my business MY business. With that message, I could attract MY target market; people who don't feel comfortable in front of the camera (and there are a lot of us out there).

As you launch your business, and receive your first paying customers or product sales, pay attention to where you thrive most and approach your business as if this is what you'll be doing every day.

The repeatable systems in place for your business (marketing, selling and fulfilling the order), will support your expansion as you thrive. Just as your kids will show signs of their talents as they get older, you will start to notice where your talents lie in your business. Pay attention to each sale and interaction as they provide vital information on where you may adjust your business tactics, increasing your enjoyment in the business, while increasing the value for your clients.

Look at all the areas of your business, and identify where you have certainty in your joy. Identify where you have strengths, and don't waste time performing actions that don't suit you.

A mom owns an agency where I work. She has her own studio. She comes in every morning and cleans the floors. Once, I asked her, "Why don't you hire someone to clean?"

She replied, "No, this is my time. I enjoy cleaning the floors. It's for me."

I was like, cleaning floors? That is why I bought a Roomba.

In your accounting, do you like collecting the checks? If you don't like that process, be open to hiring someone to handle billing. In marketing, do you like social media versus networking events? If you don't like updating social media, find someone who loves social media and ask them to help. Find where you shine, and do more of that. I personally would prefer to be networking the hell out of a room than sitting in front of my computer on social media. Your energy needs to be spent in your business doing what you love. Knowing what you love, you can decipher what you need and create the village to help you raise your business, addressing the skills you lack.

As parents, we can't be great at everything, although we strive to be. I have learned that my role as a parent has specific forms—from being a disciplinarian to teaching my son how to kick a soccer ball. I also know where I'm weakest—from not being detail-oriented (like packing the diaper bag properly) to convincing my son to eat anything outside of junk food. Fortunately, I have a wonderful partner who seems to excel at those traits! When we go to family parties, I also notice how my uncle will show my son how to have more fun and be creative, making funny noises and gestures. I have nieces and nephews (a few years older than he is) who teach him how to interact with other kids, something both my wife and I have struggled doing. I have aunts who teach him manners. This "village" is helping raise my son, showing him the skills I have a difficult time doing. The same mentality applies for building your business. Please consider creating a village to help raise your business.

BEWARE of the Hazards Ahead

Your innate business GPS tells you where to go. But there are pitfalls to beware of, and understanding these can prepare you for sharp turns as they arrive. If you can learn to anticipate traffic jams and roadblocks, they won't be in your way—or as surprising anymore.

Where Are the Results?

There will be times in your business when the hours are long, and the days are hard. You may do everything "right" in your business, but you're not reaping any immediate results.

These "pains" are not signs of failure, but signs of growth. You're going through the "growing pains" of a business.

Take potty training for example. One of the most arduous tasks a parent can undertake. You show the videos, read the books, sing the songs, constantly asking, "Do you want to use the potty?" They finally go, and you celebrate, and then they don't want to go anymore, and it's back to diapers for you! You hit a wall where you actually think your kids may never use the potty. Guess what—every human being uses the potty. It's a total fact you can bank on.

Showing up and believing in the outcome of this endeavor prepares you to have the same experience in business. Writing proposals is a great example. Sending them out and being rejected until the first person says yes. Getting a "yes" will eventually happen, you will get a job, and you may try different wording or referrals. Trust the process. Just as you teach and guide a child in any state of development, they will naturally develop into adults. This same phenomenon occurs in business.

As you do the steps outlined in this book, know that you are moving forward and that business growth is as inevitable as the growth of your kids. Take breaks when needed, but always be assured that your business IS growing, even if you're not experiencing your desired results. Time is the ultimate weight to carry, especially because in business, we want to see results immediately. As the saying goes: The majority of people overestimate what they can do in the short-term, and underestimate what they can do in the long-term. Trust that your business will develop as you continue to work in (and on) your business. Before you know it, your business will be all grown up.

Success Can Sabotage

You've gone through all the actions of launching and building your business, marketing your business effectively, providing a great value, and delivering your product/service. Now you have sales.

There is a scenario that creeps up on you at this phase. You unconsciously decide to stop marketing your business the way you used to. You stop returning phone calls, posting on social media, and going to networking events. In essence, you stop doing the actions that brought you the business. This is a new-business-owner phenomenon I'm warning you about because I experienced it in my career and saw how it could delay long-term business success.

After I had my best month ever, I got lazy and stopped going to networking events. I stopped responding to potential clients, thinking the projects were not as attractive as I wanted, and two months later, I had no business. Ouch! To get back on my feet, I went back to the grindstone. I networked again, created new packages, called people back. Sure enough, sales went up, and life was good again.

Acknowledge your success, but keep marketing and selling the ways that brought you the results you celebrate. You always need a future pipeline of prospects and referrals to keep a new business running. Don't stop your momentum because you don't think you need to market anymore. The internet means you need to market more often than ever before, reminding your customers you still exist. Consumers are constantly bombarded with information and marketing. If you stop marketing to them, don't be surprised if they forget about you—immediately.

Say you're teaching your children to walk for the first time. Day in and day out, you get them to stand up, and they fall back down. Then they stand up on their own and want to walk towards you ... only to fall back down. Finally, they stand up, face you, and take a step or two toward you. Success! After all your patience and persistence, they're walking. After you celebrate, would you think to stop practicing and teaching? After all, they've already demonstrated their ability to take a couple of steps. Of course not. You know that once your children take their first steps, your guidance and assistance is more important than ever BECAUSE they've taken their first steps. They are more likely to fall down now because they can stand.

In your business, be sure to keep your success actions

steady. Keep marketing, selling, innovating your business so that you're getting the results you desire. Celebrate your successes—and keep going.

Don't Act Like You Know Already

Being new in business and possibly your industry, you have the luxury of deriving data like a toddler. A toddler's favorite word seems to always be "Why?" For you, every question is a great question. Since you don't have much experience, your job is to extract as much information as you can to determine a course of action for your business. The majority of your questions will revolve around strategy for your business. Ask the questions of experts and other business owners. Don't be afraid of being embarrassed by asking a bad question. Asking questions can lead to innovation.

I love when "experts" in any given field tell their audiences, "You can't do it that way." I would smile and think to myself, "Well maybe YOU can't do it that way, but I'm curious to see if I can." Innovation always starts with curiosity to challenge the status quo. People who innovate question whether something can be done or not, and are willing to challenge the known of a situation with an inverse action. They don't buy into the idea that there's only one way to do anything. They're willing to explore possible alternatives.

As you grow your business, be willing to question how your industry operates and whether there is another way to be successful. Just because one tried-and-true path has been forged does not mean that another viable path can't also be forged. Question everything that doesn't feel right to you. Be willing to experiment rather than just conform to the status quo. Some of biggest accomplishments in my business came from questioning what other professionals in my industry said couldn't be done. I followed my gut which told me that there might be another way. Be courageous enough to listen to your gut. Have the curiosity of a toddler, and be willing to question.

As you implement the steps outlined throughout the book, there is no question you'll experience momentum and success in your business. The caveat is that your time and energy will become scarcer than they already were (especially being a parent). The next stage as a parent and business owner is to identify the crucial components of your company's culture; it's character and internal compass. In chapter nine, you will learn what a business needs to grow up with independence, thereby giving you the time and freedom you desire.

Chapter 9

The Culture of Your Business

"It's all about your vision and your mission."

Every book I've read, every audio program I've listened to, and every seminar I've attended on the subject of doing business told me the same thing: You need a mission and vision statement in the beginning of your business. I disagree. Every time I've attempted to craft a vision and mission statement, I struggled with creating something meaningful without yet having enough business experiences or client feedback to base my culture on.

It's just like actual parenting. Before I had my first son, I had a vague idea of what type of parent I was going to be, and how I was going to interact with my children. After experiencing parenthood firsthand, my vision went from the level of not knowing (or really filling my head with delusions of grandeur) to realizing that what mattered was the vision itself. I got caught up in the appearance of being a good dad, when the fact was that I was a good dad all along. I didn't need the validation.

That is why I advocated for you to have had experiences with building the business before going on to creating your vision, mission statements, and list of values But it's that time. It know it sounds not-so-fun, and you may have already fallen asleep after a long day with the kids even in just thinking about the brainstorming coming up, but trust me, building mission and vision statements are the framework for your whole business culture.

As a parent, you don't create mission and vision statements for your kids. It would be weird. But you have aspirations for your children. They strike you as being "a natural" at something, or you see them excel in some form of activity such as football, painting, dancing, acting, singing, or academics. As you see their talent develop, you envision how they can succeed later in life, knowing they are happy, fulfilled, and secure. The possibilities are endless, so you daydream about what they could do with their lives once they're done with schooling. Now all your activities surround this vision. You may have them practice their craft daily, making sure they give their very best. You hire the best coaches and teachers to guide them and help develop them for success. You network with people in "the industry" hoping to connect with people who can help your children reach the vision you see for them.

This process we go through with our children is a very similar to what we go through in our business. As a business owner, you're responsible for creating a vision for your child (i.e., your business). Everyone who interacts with your business (including yourself) knows where the business wants to go. Every action taken within the business has a purpose, i.e., supporting that vision of the business. This vision statement is typically stated in future tense, articulating a general company road map to your customers.

You achieve this vision by creating the second component: the mission statement. A mission statement is a statement that defines what your company delivers and why the company exists. Typically, you want this statement to be as simple as possible, so simple that a 2-year-old can understand it.

Let's take my photography business as an example.

I knew that I wanted to enjoy taking photos and make a living doing what I love. I didn't have any vision of how this would contribute to the world. Over time, I saw my company's vision develop, seeing how I made a difference in people's lives, and there was a real need out there that I could address. Many of my clients, whether they were business professionals getting head-shot photos or newlyweds getting their wedding photographed, shared a common need: They didn't like getting their photos taken. Even during events as exciting as getting married or starting a new career, their demeanors would shift to terror the moment they realized a camera was pointed in their direction. Once I saw this, I instinctually created a step-by-step process to help others relax and smile more naturally when getting their photo taken. Over time, this process improved and created predictable results. After a year in business, I had a vision for how my business could help people, and created my mission and vision statements, accompanied with a list of values.

My vision statement: To see the world smile more often.

My mission statement: To teach people how to authentically smile based on where they are.

What these statements did for me was make my business easier to talk about. The "why" was also created in my business organically without me banging my head against the wall or watching endless marketing videos explaining how to get to the why. Your vision statement connects your business to your customer.

Personality Test

The last component of the culture of your business would be the list of values in your business. The list of values determines *how* you act in your business. A consumer can be presented with two businesses offering relatively the same services, but you will get two completely different experiences. What sets them apart will be highly dependent on each company's established culture and what their values are.

Values are the principles and standards you create that determine the mannerisms of your business, articulating how anyone will execute any part of your business. Defining these values will give you and your employees clear guidelines for how to act in any situation.

My values (and Why):

- Trust: In order for to guide my clients, I have to earn their trust

- Compassion: I need to be compassionate about how they feel about getting photos taken.

- Fun: My recipe for authentically smiling is to have fun and elicit smiles naturally.

You are new to a business that you created off something you enjoyed, that passed the phase of exploration, and withstood the tests of creation, marketing, and sales. If you're struggling with creating a mission and vision statement right away, that's okay. You may be taking it too seriously or assuming they have to be perfect. The mission and vision, like your systems, will evolve as you continue to just be in your business and enjoy the process. Over time, you will see your business adding value to others, making a difference for your customers. As that happens, you'll revise your vision and mission statements. Having said that, if you DO have an idea of the vision for the company, write it down while you create your business, but understand that it'll will evolve as your business evolves.

One day, my son was playing with magnetic square and triangle tiles. They could stick together end-to-end. You could build figures by stacking the shapes together to make cubes, prisms, and more. Trying to participate in his creativity, I suggested he stack the shapes together to make one big tower. Without hesitation, he says, "No," then takes the shapes out of my hands and proceeds with his vision.

To my delight, his vision was far more creative than my boring tower idea. When he was done, he looked at me and said, "House." He had created a two-story, five-room house with triangle windows and rooftops throughout. I was so amazed, and I learned my lesson to not let my limited opinion interfere with his creativity. Whether you have a clear vision and mission for your business or not, you will be responsible for articulating them in such a way that they're easy to relate and understand. Creating this foundation of your culture will take time, but it will dramatically help you attract the right people to your business.

Benefits of Establishing Culture

Attraction of Dependable Staff

Once I defined my mission and vision statements and values, I was set. I knew where my company was going and how I was going to get there. I changed around my marketing strategies, making sure they all had my vision and values in the message. I was able to attract a subset customers (those who were nervous about getting their picture taken) who needed my help.

As the saying goes, "Birds of a feather flock together." As luck would have it, my clients would refer me to their friends, who also didn't like getting their picture taken. My referral base grew so much that I had to hire other photographers.

As I scaled up the business, hiring an assistant and other photographers, I found the process to be rather effortless. Having my mission and vision at hand, I was able to create the criteria of who would ideally represent my company. I knew the type of person I wanted and what to look for in their qualities. I treated every interview as if I were my customer, assessing whether they naturally had the character that aligned with the culture I was creating.

Many business owners come face-to-face with the stark truth that the business won't function properly without them. If they do decide to take time off, they may be welcomed back with a full inbox, countless voicemails, and "fires" to put out.

Because of this unattractive possibility, these business owners decide not to take time off and continue to work. They get burned out, just like a parent who never gets a date night. I know you are thinking, "Jeremy, why would you take us all the way to this place of building and launching our business so we can learn to get away from it?" We fall into the law of familiarity. Your days can become repetitious and predictable. Your growth is no longer exponential.

You will reach a crossroads that create a new set of possibilities within your business, and you will have some decisions to make that will give you more time, and make you more money. Here are a couple of likely scenarios that you may face that bring you to these crossroads:

Scenario 1: You are a business owner who specializes in a specific service with one employee, YOU. Over time, your business grows, and you find yourself with more customers, and no time to fulfill your sales. You find that you're turning away potential business because you simply don't have the time or energy to provide the quality of work you demand out of your business. You know you have a great service to provide and want to help as many people as you can.

Scenario 2: You are the same business owner in Scenario 1, but this time, you're able to hire one or two people to help with day-to-day duties that you don't have time for and/or you're not as skilled at as they are. You find yourself wanting to step away from the business to take a small break. You manage to calculate that, with the staff you have, you'll be able to get away for a while, and your staff will be able to manage the business until you get back. How will you know your staff will provide the service to your expectations for the business (without you being there to oversee them)?

Both scenarios are real scenarios I've experienced in my businesses, and the solutions have been found in the culture of my business. As in Scenario 1, at a certain point, you will have more business, and if time is the finite resource, then you need to leverage other people's time. To leverage other people's time, you need to have an established culture for the sake of consistency. Therefore, culture is the moral standard of your business, but it's also what propels you forward in business expansion.

When you decide you want to hire someone, you're more likely to find the right person by making sure the interviewee has the same values as your company. If your vision and mission are strong, you can attract people who *want* to work for your company. They will seek you out, wanting to be part of a vision that matches their own vision. They want to work in an environment that shares the same values they do. Likewise, you'll also be able to turn away people who don't share the same values. You can potentially avoid misalignment and letting go of an employee with a clear vision and established culture.

Decisions Become Obvious

When a business is clear about its vision, mission, and values, all actions have purpose and direction. Everyone knows where the business is going. When faced with a scenario, an individual in the business will have guidelines of how to respond. You can also change any system to match your culture.

Take the people my business attracts, for example. They dislike getting their photos taken. To remedy this, I changed every system of my business to make sure the client felt safe and comfortable throughout the entire process. That included having a planning session over the phone to discuss what the photo shoot would entail, describing my philosophy of photography, and how that affects them. I changed my fulfillment processes by creating video tutorials to send out before the photo session so clients can better prepare and feel at ease knowing what to expect. I gave the clients step by step instructions of what to expect next, making sure they knew there would be no surprises, and they could relax, trusting I was on top of everything. I'd also make sure to be as thorough as possible, demonstrating I knew my craft and anticipating any scenario that could happen.

Empower Employees/Ensure Clients

Your culture gives your employees the freedom to make their own decisions. You've given them the framework of conduct and ethics needed to ensure they will do "the right thing" when the time comes. Just as you would watch your children go off to college on their own, you can take the vacation from your business knowing you have done everything you need to make sure they will be okay.

Your clients may look to you as the face of the business, but, ultimately, what they care about most is a good result. If you can ensure them that your employees can provide them that result, then the pressure is off of you to provide that service every time. No one can ever do it as well as you can, but you need the freedom to grow your business instead of being in the weeds with each new client. At a certain point, doing the actual work is a waste of your time. Creating systems helps you add more value to more people.

Bringing it back to premise of this book, let's see how setting up our business culture parallels our parenting culture!

Mind Your Manners

As your kids get older, you anticipate they'll have experiences you won't be there for and won't be able to guide them through firsthand. You send them off to school, daycare, or to hang out with their friends, trusting they'll make the "right" decisions when faced with any scenario. But how do you ensure they know what the right decisions are? As a parent, you teach them a code of conduct, a list of guidelines that will determine how they respond when presented with a situation. These guidelines might include :

- *Don't talk to strangers.*
- *Don't do drugs.*
- *Protect yourself at all times.*
- *Live adventurously.*
- *Follow your heart.*
- *Respect your elders.*
- *Be good and have fun.*
- *Do your best.*

Every parent has advice they give to their children about how to behave and how to approach life. When looked at closely, this advice emphasizes what's most important for the parents to pass on to their kids. Your hope is that these guidelines provide your children with the moral awareness when you're not around to guide them. From an outsider's perspective, you can also tell how someone else's kids were raised, and what their parents emphasized by looking at their actions or reactions to events.

In your business, you will experience events you may not have anticipated or prepared for. In the event you need to hire staff to help you, you anticipate that they'll also encounter these scenarios. Go back to Scenario 2 above where you need to train staff so you can go off and do other marketing or sales efforts. How your staff will act (without your supervision) will be based on the guidelines (i.e., the company culture) you create ahead of time.

Not Easy, but Worth It

As simple as this concept may seem, establishing culture isn't just about statements and values, just as kids behaving isn't just about a one-time lesson. There will be days when your business throws a fit. In other words, you're off your game like agreeing to a project for the money when you knew it was the wrong project. Or you cut corners to meet deadlines knowing the value you offer would suffer. You are so busy, you don't sleep, and you don't return emails. The short of it is we make culture mistakes in our business based on circumstance. You then have to go in and take the time to fix these lapses.

What's important is for you to flex your parenting muscles of repetition and consistency, ensuring that your message and teachings are embedded throughout the DNA of your business. When your business deviates from its guidelines or your employees don't make the "right decisions," you have to realign them both back to your vision and mission. Remind your employees of the values that make them unique. Over time, your business and its employees will start internalizing the guidelines that define your business.

Culture is *the* foundation of any business and must be established for your business to "grow up" on its own. In that culture, you determine where you are working *in* your business or *on* your business. This distinction is for business owners to make, and it will change as their business evolves.

We define our art through our products and services, and we learn how to sell it. With an established culture, we can go back to the imagination and exploration, expanding our own talents and creativity based on our joy. What evolves from this return to joy is new products and services (in other words: more income streams). If you have all your necessities met, you get to play the game of innovation. You don't have to worry too much about surviving. But you do need to keep an eye on the whole picture, while trusting your team enough to build more businesses, concepts, and products.

Chapter 10

Protecting What You Built

*"How to let go of the reins,
and watch your business survive ... and thrive."*

Being in your business day in and day out, you don't see from an outside perspective how established you really are, or how much you have grown over time. Just like you vet the teachers who'll interact with your kids, or the babysitter who'll watch them after school, when you leave your business in the hands of employees, you want to feel safe with them at the controls. By doing so, you're doing your due diligence to ensure the safety of your business while you're away, whether to build other companies, generate additional income streams, or carve out free time for a vacation (what a concept!). The decisions you make in protecting your business ensure that your sales and marketing systems are efficient to bring in new business, and your brand continues to have a presence in the marketplace.

I spoke about how launching and running a business, in its simplest form, was comprised of three systems: creating a product/service, marketing/selling the product/service, and fulfilling the order. When born, both business and children, you address their basic needs. As they grow up, there are more variables that have to be considered beyond basic needs. You have to consider safety, survival, and independence.

Without these core elements, they'll become over-dependent on you for life and won't be fully realized in their potential or individuality. A business can have its own life even when you let go of the reins, and it can survive and thrive as long as you protect it.

Protection

As a parent, I make many choices to ensure my kids are at once safe and learning to survive on their own in the future. While thoughts of harm can be very uncomfortable to think about, especially regarding my children, being prepared is better than the naïve belief that no misfortune will ever befall you.

Decisions around protection and safety of my kids' well-being started out with what car seats and strollers had the best safety ratings, scheduling vaccinations, and SIDS prevention. As they got older, I looked at different life-insurance plans and college-savings plans. Being in the Bay Area, I also had environmental considerations. I noticed how unprepared we were as a family in the event of natural disasters.

From a business perspective, you have to think about how you'll parent your business in a similar fashion, making decisions that will better protect your business and ensure your business can thrive in the short and long term. You may not like considering the "bad" that can happen in your business, but you have to be aware of the possibilities, and prepare as best you can before they occur.

My second son was born during the writing of this book. One night, I woke up to the innocent sounds of a crying newborn, helpless in his crib. Right after he settled back in, an earthquake shook our house. The tremor was a relatively small one (considering how common they are in California), so I wasn't too concerned for my safety. My children didn't wake from the tremor, but I couldn't go back to sleep. I played different scenarios in my head of what I would do if a bigger quake hit.

"Let's see," I thought, "since my wife is right next to the baby, I'll make sure she gets him and heads for cover. I'll run to Sebastian's room, grab him, and head for shelter as well. Should we need to evacuate, I would probably only have two minutes to pack a few necessities. But wait! We should already have a bag prepared. I better do that in the morning. But what if there's an earthquake while I'm working, and my wife is at home with the kids? The cellphone lines might be blocked, and we wouldn't have any way of communicating. We might need a discussion about that as well ...."

Two hours later, I'd managed to go back to sleep only to have my two-year-old instructing me that it was time to wake up.

Look at your business like your family. Anticipate the extraneous "ground-shaking" conditions that can rattle the vulnerabilities or weaknesses in your business. Incorporate your business (or at least see a business lawyer to discuss the various options), use contracts (and if you pull them from the internet, run them by a lawyer), and take on business insurance. I highly recommend hiring a lawyer on retainer to make sure you are in compliance with regulatory laws. You wouldn't cut corners with the safety of your children, so why would you do that with your business? Whatever needs to happen to protect your business, you're far better off being prepared BEFORE disaster happens rather than after. You also can operate with the peace of mind, knowing your business is protected and that you've covered all the bases to the best of your ability.

So, what can potentially happen to break your business-owner bliss?

Altercations

As your business grows and expands, you will inevitably get "misalignment" with a customer or two. Your business will encounter an unhappy person who disagrees with how you conduct your business or is unhappy with your service. If immediate resolution is not an option, these customers might make their dissatisfaction known in a very public manner. They may argue with you, possibly write a bad review online, or in a worst-case scenario, threaten to take legal action.

These situations come about to push you to take a step back and evaluate whether you're misaligned with your vision and mission. Try to understand the legitimacy of a customer's negative opinion and see if there's room to improve your business. Or, check in with yourself (and the business) to see if you might be doing something wrong or inappropriate. But by no means should you take their feedback personally or as a personal attack against you. From time to time, we are going to encounter people who challenge our value and worth, and we need to stand up to them and stay firm on our price, practices, and boundaries. Just like when a kid wants something, and you have decided no, and then you hedge a little to open discussion. And then immediately you regret it because the kid pushes for more and throws a fit on you when you try to shut the situation down.

In my photography business, altercations are the perfect example of why I started to make contracts mandatory. I have come to find that you can do everything "right," develop great rapport with your client, leave feeling satisfied from a project, and still experience a worst-case scenario, e.g., your supplier screws up quality control, or your client changes their mind about what they want and you have to start over. In fact, those instances are when you might be the most vulnerable in your business, when everything goes so well that you let your guard down. I let my guard down just one and experienced a costly mistake.

There was a last-minute wedding job where the photographer backed out. I was brand-new and said I could help out where I could. I sent the client a link to my website so they could review my work. On the day of the event, they were happy-go-lucky. I didn't even have them sign the contract because they were all pre-occupied. After the wedding, I sent them a preview of the photos, which they approved of. After sending the entire album, they changed their tune and suddenly wanted all their money back, saying the pictures were not up to their expectations. My error was that I didn't follow up with them after they'd reviewed my website to ensure they liked my work. I thought it was a great experience, but then at the end, when everything was said and done, I had to refund the money and give them the photos. Because of that example, I created protections systems for my business and began issuing contracts with every photo session, no matter what. I've even lost business because clients have refused to sign the contract. I also vet clients before the job and make sure that they've seen my work, and that my work fits what they want.

Despite the loss in business, I would rather say no to the revenue than put my company in a vulnerable position. On the flip side, I feel the freedom now that my business is protected, and I don't have to worry about any harm to its bottom line. I'm confident I can put my attention elsewhere, knowing my business is safe and secure.

"Yes" Is a Trap

When we start out in business, we want to say yes to every opportunity that comes knocking on our door, hoping to make money for the business. When I started photography, I said yes to every project that came my way no matter if I could do it or not, or whether I liked the client.

In my first business as a life coach, I was an ambitious 19-year-old, ready to take on the world's problems one client at a time. My positive energy and good intentions felt like I could conquer anything. I met a gentleman who had seen my business card on a local coffee-shop bulletin board. He reached out to me, seeking coaching, and strategies for his struggling business. After disclosing all of his business challenges, I knew I wasn't experienced or educated enough to provide viable strategies, but I decided to accept his business and figure out a way.

After one meeting, the client could see right through my inexperience and started berating me. He said that he had serious problems and didn't have the luxury to waste time. Even after I apologized, he said my apologies won't help his situation. He made a point to say that he would do everything in his power to make sure people knew I was a fraud, and that no one would ever hire me.

Needless to say, that experience shaped my future in business. The way to get out of the "Yes" trap is being very specific and clear about what you can deliver. Know what value your product or service provides, and let the client determine whether they want that service. You can add more, and learn more, but stay in the certainty of your core skill or product. While it's commendable to believe in yourself and your versatility, or that many elements of your service can be learned as you go, be very clear about your value, and let the client make the decision if they feel you are qualified for what they need.

In my photography business, I made it a point to turn away clients knowing certain projects weren't a good fit for my services. I was able to refer these opportunities to someone more qualified and in sync with what the project entailed. Moving on and keeping yourself in the right alignment with your vision as a business owner is key. At this stage of your business, be efficient with your time and connect with clients who align with your company. Even though I turned away potential money, I knew I was doing the right thing and providing the value to the right clients.

As a parent, I see my son being easily swayed by "sugar persuasion." Whenever I would ask him to do something, he may comply or resist. I'm well aware that if I really wanted him to do something, all I'd have to do is bribe him with candy and cookies. He'll smile, be the perfect angel of compliance, and get his reward for his actions. Kids respond very predictably to pleasure. The idea of saying yes to some type of pleasure is easy. Kids do this all the time. It's when they say no to some form of desired pleasure that they start demonstrating independence and character. You may see this typically in kids in later elementary grades or pre-teens. They start to understand the consequences to saying yes, especially if you allow them to suffer them sometimes.

When you start out in business, your focus is on survival, which means generating income and revenue. Saying yes to sales is easy because it meets your need to survive. But as your business grows up, your need to survive will decrease and your ability to align your business to the right customers increases. Your purpose becomes the focus and your actions adjust accordingly.

Your Business's Self-Esteem

However your "misalignment" shows up, see it as an opportunity to examine a concept I call "your business's self-esteem." If, after you "check-in" with your business, you find that you've done everything you believe is right, and that you're adding value to your customer, stand up for your business, and rest in the confidence knowing that you ARE "right." No amount of threats or demands will deter you from what you believe in. You remain confident in your actions, certain that your business has lived up to its mission and vision, and that you're comfortable with the outcomes, however they may show up.

Your courage to stand up for your actions demonstrate your business's self-esteem and that it can grow on its own. Having this characteristic also gives you the certainty to turn away business, and prevent "misalignments" from occurring in the first place. During the sales process of your business, your self-esteem will be your compass, aligning you with the RIGHT customers rather than every customer that inquires for your service. If you know someone isn't a good fit for what you do, you have the power to refer them to someone else that can better serve their needs. You're clear about what your value is, and how to spot *your* clients from the rest. In fact, the moment you become a real business is when you say "no" to potential business.

Then you can do what I typically did after one business was up and running: Create the next business!

The Evolution

Having more time to create new spinoffs seems like a concept too farfetched for me to even bring up at this juncture, but I assure you it's the natural progression of a business owner to start another business. Creating a successful business is like having your first child pass their second year. At some point, you miss the excitement and growth in the beginning and entertain the concept of having another. If you have covered all the bases for your current business's growth such that it's healthy and protected, you can look to starting another business and creating more revenue streams.

Before you take that next leap, step back, and look at how far you've come. From the moment you became a first-time parent to today—see how you've evolved. You've experienced new levels of joy. You've developed new talents and passions that you may never have known existed. You've expanded your scope of possibilities. All of this was possible because of you.

Once I had this realization, I saw the world differently. I realized how anything is truly possible with time and persistence. Whatever I could envision could be mine to experience. I got to play the game on my terms, knowing that all my experiences have led me to this point.

The Game We All Play

The *game* I'm referring to is the game of life, a very interesting game that most people don't know how to play. Here is a game where you're in charge of setting up the rules, the participants in the game, the standards of how to keep score, the time limit for each segment, and every other variable that the game has to offer ... and YET ... most people still seem to fail at winning this game. How is this possible?!

Once I was able to experience business success, I started to see this game more clearly. I realized how I could do what I love and how the money would come. When money came, I could dictate my own schedule. When I controlled how much money I made in a year, I could "win" the game of life. With this clarity, I created more segments of this game.

This game of life is yours to win, should you choose to. I believe that most people don't win this game because they don't believe in their abilities, or they don't believe there's another level of possibility for them. They set themselves up to make ends meet and experience glimpses of joy to help them get by. Rarely do they challenge themselves to expand beyond their comfort zones.

But as parents, you've chosen to expand. Before you were parents, there was nothing that guaranteed your success as a parent. You weren't born under the right star, knowing for a fact that you'd be a great parent. There was no prophecy controlling your destiny. You took a risk and bet on yourself that you'd figure it all out as you went along. And you did! You found a new level of confidence and ability through which you evolved into the person you are today.

I can make a fair assumption that you are NOT the person you were before having children. Children provide you with experiences that change your perspective on life. Children help you evolve as human beings, strengthening your talents and beliefs in yourself. Children test your threshold of tolerance and teach you patience and humility. By having children, you reach a whole new level of being.

Levels of Life

In the beginning of this book, I talked about having an "itch" that doesn't seem to go away. This itch referred to your curiosity to running your own business, exploring your potential and discovering your capabilities. We've "leveled up" our lives by being parents, creating life, and sacrificing what was familiar to us in favor of exploring the unknown. In doing so, we've pushed our limits beyond anything we could imagine, from testing our functionality on no sleep to convincing our children to eat anything even remotely healthy.

A business has the potential to provide a similar experience of up-leveling you to more than being just a parent. We wear many hats as individuals: spouse, parent, friend, employee, boss, etc. You can be all those roles, rather than identify with any single one. That balance makes everyone in your life touched by all parts of you. Imagine that finding your joy can kick off a whole series of events for others in your life. Getting curious about what's possible and taking action sets off a series of fortuitous events. Doing all the steps in this book will guide you to achieving that next level.

As a business owner, I've had my share of highs and lows. During my lows, I would wonder whether I should get a regular job, knowing I needed to provide security for my family. Before making the decision to close the business, I vented to a successful entrepreneur about the struggles of running a business while having kids. I complained that all my models of successful business-owners had kids *after* their companies succeeded. Before I could get another word in, she interrupted me by saying that her mom became a successful business owner after she's had her. She added that she was an entrepreneur because of her mom's success and influence.

That conversation convinced me to let go of my limitations of parenting and business building. It also introduced a question about my legacy and influence to my children. "What type of example am I setting for my kids if I don't go for my dreams and aspirations?" I thought. "How would I react if I saw my children accept less than they could be?"

By exploring the levels in your life, you create the opportunity for the people around you to explore their levels. You become the example they may look towards for inspiration. Your successes become their successes. And as Marianne Williamson said in her famous speech:

> "...as we let our own light shine, we unconsciously give other people permission to do the same. As we are liberated from our own fear, our presence automatically liberates others".

What you do today with your life affects the people closest to you and your family. Level up your life by adding the role of business owner to your collection of hats. Let your courage and curiosity influence your kin to go for their dreams and not hold back.

I've observed how parents can get caught up that their identity as a parent. All their actions are directed to fulfilling that one identity. It makes me reflect on my life. "Am I a good dad if I don't carry around this identity of just being a parent?" I wonder. "Does that identity make me a better or worse parent?"

I strive to be the best parent I can be, but I believe that being a parent is one of many roles I have in this life and doesn't have to be my sole identity. Please understand that I don't think that parents who identify themselves as only being parents (and nothing else) is bad or wrong. I believe in the possibility that you can experience other levels of joy and fulfillment (in ADDITION to being a parent). Whether you decide to have kids or to start a business, the point is to find new levels of joy and happiness in your growth as an individual. The possibilities are endless if you're willing to step outside what you know. Dare to dream of what's possible in your world, and the world will conspire to help you fulfill those dreams.

You're going to protect your children and your business. These are gifts in your life, and you won't take them for granted or treat them haphazardly. In parenting as in business ownership, people will tell us horrible notions that might worry us for a beat. As parents, we do our own research, confer with other parents to get our answers, and draw our own conclusions as long as we don't panic. Panic is terrible for parenting and business alike.

So what am I saying? People will try to tell you all kinds of crazy crap about running a business. I've heard them all. Knowing all the crap in advance can keep you from feeding into paranoia or panic, and allow you to stay true to the intuitions you have about the business you built.

Chapter 11

Business Misconceptions

"Building your armor against
the myths and the misconceptions"

There's a fair share of conventional "wisdoms" regarding business that are simply disguised misconceptions. I challenge these misconceptions because they can overwhelm you and stop you from continuing on your business path. As we near the end of this book, some of you may still be hesitant about starting your business. You're at the edge of taking action but can't get yourself to cross over and commit to at least exploring. I can guarantee one or more of these issues are holding you back from taking that first step to finding your joy and exploring your ideal business.

These misconceptions come from my experiences and from observing and interviewing hundreds of entrepreneur-parents like yourself. Without all the noise from this survey or that branding course, I'm providing you with a well-rounded perspective of what running a business COULD be like, and get you to take action.

I wish someone had made this same list for parenting and owned it like I am about to do for you with business. I could've gotten back countless hours of time spent "researching" parenting. "Do you choose sleep training with the Ferber method, letting them cry it out, or do you run in every five minutes to rock them?" "Do you enroll them in a Reggio Emilia preschool, or a small homespun daycare?" "Should I vaccinate my newborns?" "Is formula better than breast milk?" "Do I let others hold my newborn?" "Do I let my kids co-sleep with us?" "What foods do I feed my toddler?" "Do I let my toddlers watch TV or go online?" "What methods of discipline are most effective in a toddler (timeout, yelling, spanking)?" and I would've stockpiled all the sleep I needed to prepare for a household of small children. *Yawn.* It's enough to make you want to just turn on the TV, and let them eat the remote. Finding bona fide wisdom is part of the challenge. Drowning out all the horror of what *could* happen if you make the "wrong parenting decision" was even worse.

Misconception #1: Everyone Has It easier Than You and/or Is More Educated in Business.

When evaluating your abilities to start a business, you compare yourself to your peers or your competition, and see how they seem to have everything in order, how they were "born under the right star," and how they had an easier time starting than you, so why bother, right? You make the immediate assumption that they went to that school you never thought to apply to, or they had some incredible coach you could never afford.

All you can do, in the meantime, is watch all the free videos you can find online about how to build an email list or make a YouTube channel. You figure, at that rate, you may have a business to build a life ... in ten years.

These feelings of lack have some similarities to being a first-time parent. At some point in your anticipation of parenthood, you sang a similar tune of fear and dread, feeling unprepared or incapable. You watched other people brilliantly swaddle and rock their babies, and feed them pureed organic sweet potatoes and think, holy cow, I'm never going to live up to these expectations. So how did that play out for you? Your kid ended up fine even if he ate Pringles for breakfast and fell asleep under the kitchen table. Like I've been saying throughout this book, your parenting gives you an edge in business, because you've already been through this doubt and fear.

You didn't have the life experience or the master's degree in parenting that guaranteed you success as a parent—and your kid turned out not just great, but awesome.

Shift #1: Leverage What You DO Have

In business, what you lack in "business education," you compensate with persistence, focus, and discipline. If you don't have an answer to a business question, your parenting skills will ensure that you'll find a way or figure it out. I'm not saying that a business education won't help but not having a business background doesn't destine you for failure. Parents have an uncanny ability to harness pure *will* and resourcefulness when necessary. When you forget to bring a diaper, you'll find the courage to ask a fellow parent for a diaper, or you'll exercise your creativity with some paper towels and duct tape until you get home.

There is a phrase that helps me whenever I feel "unqualified" to do something: *Every master was once a disaster.* Creating a business is nothing more than a learned skill, which is something that parents continually do as their kids grow up. With all the "lack" you feel you have, there is far more working in your favor than you realize as you start a new business.

Misconception #2: My industry Is Oversaturated.

Once you decide on a business idea, you'll research your competition and realize there are more people working in that field or industry than just you. Intimidation sets in, and you question why you should even start, since there are so many others, already established, providing the same value you do. Then you ask yourself, "Does the world need another (fill in your business idea)."

If this doesn't hit home with you, you're very fortunate. I asked myself that question in several businesses, including my photography business. Consider my situation. I started my photography business just as companies integrated camera technology to phone products. With improvements, the camera phones were so advanced that in certain circumstances, you couldn't tell if a photo was taken from a camera phone or a $10,000 camera setup.

It seemed like anyone with a camera phone could now become an amateur photographer. I'm pretty sure that you couldn't get into a more saturated market than what I was facing.

If you're able to step back and look at any industry objectively, you'll see that every market has "oversaturation." I'm sure that your industry isn't unique to this phenomenon. The fear of oversaturation is the fear of whether there's enough business to go around or whether you'll be able to generate sales with so much competition.

Shift #2: Individuality Removes Competition

How I dealt with such a daunting thought was by focusing on my unique contribution to my industry rather than "the conditions of industry." Focus on your individual style and on the flavor that your company brings, and you'll see who that attracts.

Having oversaturation doesn't discount the value you can provide. Your brand will be defined better because you see a need that isn't being met. Oversaturation means your product or service must deliver more distinguished value so it stands out from the pack.

For example, you have a kid in sports. Say they're on the soccer team. There could be kids bigger than your kid (I know, I was the little kid), and that forced me to find another definable skill like ball-handling.

Take this to another level and look at NBA star Steph Curry of the Golden State Warriors. He is not 6'9 and quick. He's 6'2, which is short for the NBA. He leveraged his ability to shoot quickly to distinguish himself and changed basketball in the process. He made the three-pointer relevant. During scouting, he was told he was too short and had weak ankles. Now he is a two-time MVP champion.

An oversaturated market gives me opportunity to exercise my own individuality and focus on how I'm different than everyone else. This emphasis is what made my brand so successful. I focused more on my message and what I wanted to contribute to this industry.

Once my message was set, I realized how easy attracting clients could be. I never had a hard time finding business in what, to my mind, was the most "oversaturated" industry out there.

Misconception #3: Self-Made Success

There's a prestige attached to tales of self-made success. You hear stories about how someone was brought up from nothing, and through their own willpower and determination, they rose up to become more than what anyone else ever could have ever anticipated ... all on their own.

To me, being "self-made" is the biggest misconception there is in business. Research the history of any proclaimed "self-made" success, and I will show you contributions by others that made their success happen.

Even if you showed me a self-made business success, I wouldn't consider that success much of an achievement. Yes, you can say you succeeded on your own, but how much more exciting and fulfilling would the experience be if you were to share your journey and succeed with others? If fact, you should strive to NOT be a "self-made" success in business.

Shift # 3: Create a Village

Most business owners, when starting out, tend to think they need to do EVERYTHING for their business, mostly due to lack of initial capital. What you lack in capital resources, you make up for with your time. But once you drop the baggage of needing to be a "self-made success," you begin to include how others can help, thus, creating opportunities for work and growth.

What I've found is that when you have a team to help you, success comes much quicker because you're leveraging other people's time and energy toward a common goal. So, you're basically doing more in less time. Strive to not be a self-made success, incorporating others to your business and asking for help.

You don't have to be a genius or superhero to be great in business. Be who you are, and create a team. People are not born good in business. Talent needs to be nurtured and guided. College students don't just land in pro-sports. People may think they're gifted, but the outside world has no idea how many coaching and training sessions their parents paid for (and you may be nodding your head right now), and games they had to play to get to that status. You invest money and time as parents, and the kids invest time and often their social lives.

No one is self-made. You're going to need help at some point. You didn't make the internet or the computers you are using, or the electricity. Employ some help.

Misconception #4: A Business Will Take Up All of Your Time.

"A business will give you the freedom to set your own hours; you're free to work whatever 20 hours a day you'd like." The first time I heard this statement, I was completely engulfed with photography and was probably working at least 15 hours a day, seven days a week. Here was the catch: I CHOSE to work those hours because I enjoyed photography so much.

Most people who work tirelessly at their business generally have a vision or a passion they focus on that gets them to work such insane hours. Most of the time, their hours are dictated by obsession or by necessity. Since you're just starting out in business, I would guess that you may not NEED to work such hours.

Business owners who work long hours out of necessity tend to wear many hats in the business. I see individual business owners handle sales, marketing, accounting, fulfillment, quality control, innovation, operations, etc. Their days are filled with website design, social media updates, content creation, invoicing and billing, inbounds sales leads, product/service fulfillment ... all of it equating to *busy* work.

Shift #4: Leverage

As business owners, you'll tend to believe that no one can do certain tasks better than you, and that others won't care about your business as much as you do. That said, I would guess that many of the tasks you take on could be outsourced to someone else or replaced with some technology, freeing up your time for more of the important tasks in your business. There are tasks that will take up a great deal of your time, but might be faster for others.

A couple of tasks in my business that take up much of my time are creating proposals and billing clients. So, I decided to outsource the work to someone else. This person took a fraction of time to do all the work, saving me time to do other tasks. And her fees were paid for (and then some) with all the new business my newfound time allowed me to generate.

Even if money is tight in the beginning of your business, and you think you can't afford to hire someone, I would suggest that you explore the idea anyways and, see what you can find. Interns, online personal assistants/virtual assistants, and technology are all viable ways to outsource some of your tasks. The point is to prioritize the tasks in your business that NEED your attention over the tasks that can be hired out to someone else.

I had mentioned in a previous chapter than, once my son was born, I ended up cutting two workdays from my schedule, limiting how much time I was actually in the business. The reality is that you can be as involved or as passive with your business as you choose. Your priorities are will dictate how you schedule your day. I'm here to tell you that starting a business and staying connected with your family are possible; I'm living proof.

My second son was born in the midst of my writing this book even as I maintained my photography business and took care of my two-year-old, who inspired me to write this book in the first place. My newborn became a fixture in the Skype sessions with my book coach. (I think she was less excited when I would show up to the coaching sessions alone.)

You'll never convince me that you can't maintain the quality of fulfillment in your life, both personal and professionally, and run a successful business. A business does not have to take over your life. This solution is a simple answer. Revert back to Misconception #3, and ask for help. That way, you can create the schedule that will keep you fulfilled in the long term.

Misconception # 5: "Overnight" Success

Meet the cousin to the "self-made success." I dislike this label more because the media over-exaggerates such stories to grab more eyeballs. The idea that a business has become an "overnight" success is absolutely ridiculous. You'll never find any actual truth to it in any legitimate business literature, interviews, or TED Talks.

Think about it. When has a successful person admitted they were an "overnight success"? You ask any business owner about their "overnight" success, and they will tell about the years of work and sacrifice they endured to find their success. It's three-quarters of the fun of victory.

Shift #5: Prepare for a Marathon, not a Sprint.

As we've seen in previous chapters, a business is like a child. If I were to tell you how lucky you were to have such a well-behaved child created overnight, you'd laugh in my face. I'm only seeing the end-result of tireless parenting. You know all the challenges you've had with your child, the fights, the failures, and victories over years that created this well-behaved human being.

Overnight success is a myth. The good news is that, now that you know it, you're free to take your time. There's no rush or pressure to achieve such "status." You can live your life, enjoy your process, and succeed in all areas, from family to business.

As a parent, you know that time flies much quicker than it used to. Your kids are growing up quickly, as will your business. Who knows? In a few short years, you'll be asked how you became such an overnight business success. See how you react!

Misconception #6: It Takes Money to Make Money.

I can't tell you how many times people have told me they hadn't started their business because they didn't have capital. This idea that you NEED to have money to start a business is not completely true. I concede that having money helps, and you can get to where you want to faster with extra capital. But as you're starting out, rarely will an influx of capital be the determining factor for your success or failure.

Shift #6: Leverage other resources other than money

If you think you need money to start a business, use your parenting skills, and be the ultimate creative problem solver. You know that you don't need to come up with an elegant solution, but a results-based one that will get the job done. If you don't have enough milk for your child's cereal, mix the remaining milk with some water. If you don't have a tissue to wipe your kid's nose, your sleeve will do just fine. If you have a power outage and need to make dinner, order out or make something cold for them to eat.

If you don't have money to start your business, you can get a loan from a bank, look at private investors like friends and family, or leverage your skill sets as payment for services that you currently need. When my business was building momentum, I knew I needed the essentials of marketing, such as a website and logo. I also wanted to make sure that these items reflected the brand I wanted to portray. Unfortunately, I didn't have the money to invest in a unique website. At the time, building your website for free online wasn't a service yet, and I didn't have the luxury of time to learn coding and to build my own.

I got resourceful and ended up using my photography skills as payment for these items. I got a website from a friend and a logo design from a relative. My payment was photography services. No money was exchanged.

I know a parent who had a great idea for a business but had money challenges. To fulfill her bakery goods orders, she needed special equipment but didn't have the money to buy it. Being a mom, she created a couple of solutions. She knew that her family had tried her products before, so she started with them. She presented a plan for a small loan to purchase the equipment so she could fulfill larger orders. The plan also spelled out her loan repayment schedule. Because fortune smiles on action, one of her family members gave her the loan. Her plan completely worked. She purchased the equipment, fulfilled her orders, and paid back the loan on the schedule she created.

Misconception #7: The Customer Is Always Right (and Always Knows What They Want).

Oh, yes, I'm going there. Business owners fear altercations and disagreements with customers. You always hear, "The customer is always right," which means that you have to do whatever the customer wants to make them happy.

I'm here to tell you that the customer is not always right. In fact, the customer rarely knows what they want! So how can they be right? Before you decide I've completely lost my mind, stay with me, and see if I can provide you with a sound and healthy perspective.

Shift #6: Feedback Helps—but Doesn't Control—Alignment

To provide you with more perspective, a great businessman named Henry Ford (founder of the Ford Motor Company) had a wonderful perspective regarding customer feedback said:

*"If I had asked people what they wanted,
they would have said faster horses."*

Most people don't really know what they want or need. I've experienced this phenomenon in my photography business.

In the beginning, I thought people knew what they wanted, so I would provide them with à la carte menus, detailing any and every service their heart desired. Rarely did I get any sales with this approach. I quickly understood that customers relied on me to tell them what they wanted or needed. They expected me to create their structure, in terms of the amount of time they'd need, how many photos they'd get, and what the total price would be—all in the simplest presentation.

Don't let the fear of confrontation of any kind, whether it is a dissatisfied customer or someone balking at your rates, prevent you from ever starting a business. That's like saying you don't want kids because you're afraid you two will fight. Confrontations happen in business. They're part of the process, not a sign of failure. Knowing that you've done your part to create a valuable business experience for your customers, you have to trust that your vision is tailored to what they'll want/need. Those not in alignment with your business practices and vision will fall away.

Think of this list of misconceptions and their solutions as the armor you'll need to venture into the world as a business owner, and explore what you can uniquely offer so that you can prosper. We all think we need so much information to make any start, but simplicity and faith are the key ... in both parenting and business.

Chapter 12

Are You Still Breathing?

"Start with joy, and build out from there."

Each chapter of this book has taken you through the different stages of building a business; from finding your joy all the way up to preparing your business to work without you. This book's primary goal has been to provide you with perspective about entrepreneurship while simplifying what business building entails. In this simplicity, you take action, find your joy and move forward with your 4 hours a week to explore your ideas and beyond.

It's the journey of your business, and the enjoyment along the way that ultimately matters—just as in like parenting. I can't emphasize that enough. Throughout the book, I have compared parenting to running a business and asked you to see how many of your life experiences have profound similarities to business development. As you experience hiccups in your business, continue to look at how you handled a rough moment in parenting, and apply those lessons to your business. This book is not intended to be radical or whimsical ... the "parenting a business" method works over and over again. I've seen it first hand, and taught this approach to many others.

In the course of this book, you've covered a lot of ground, learning step by step how to analyze where you are and start a business. Let's step back and reflect on what you've learned to reinforce a positive perspective on building a fruitful and lucrative business.

We began by your exploring an answer to the question, "Why am I curious about starting a business?" You realized that, despite all your obligations, you couldn't ignore the nagging desire to launch an innovative enterprise. You courageously looked at the "why" head-on and engaged in all the possibilities of starting a business.

As parents, we face a wide range of events that challenge us, taking our focus and time. You learned that circumstances in life do not equate to success or failure. No matter what, our children grow up. Making yourself aware of these challenges gives you the leverage you need to strategize your resources effectively, and build a thriving business.

Along with the "why," we addressed how the beginnings of a business involves the discovery of joy. Make this process easy on yourself. Find joy and come back to it. Joy is the key ingredient to the consistency and attention needed in your business. Joy gives you the desire to keep going and evolve. It increases your motivation to take action. In finding your joy, you saw that you don't need a big time investment to start. If you spent a minimum of 4 hours a week on your business, finding your joy and getting resourceful, you are that much more likely to convert that enthusiasm into a business.

When I discuss this topic of joy to budding business owners, I typically meet with a sense of resistance at any attempt to find joy. Needing to find joy means you that you don't have it right now. When they realize and accept that truth, they feel moved to find their joy. Understanding the vitality of joy, business owners fear they will never find or discover what that is.

If you too share this sense of hesitation, take a breath, and relax. Finding joy doesn't have to be overnight. Sometimes, joy takes a while to discover. As long as you're actively searching, trust that you will eventually discover it.

The "how" in finding your joy is up to you. I have two suggestions that have been proven to work (with execution and time).

First, reflect on your memories of when you had the most fun doing a task, or when you felt like time stopped and you were in the flow. And before you knew it, the day is over. Remember what part of those activities lit up your mind and heart, and see if you still sense some joy now as you relive those memories.

Second, try new activities. If you find yourself stuck in discovering joy, branch out into areas of the unknown. Step out of your comfort zones, and explore new activities that "could" spark your interest. These activities can be as random as arts-and-crafts, group exercise classes, participating in a Toastmasters speaking event, doing group theater, taking an online course in a subject you've been curious about, or creative writing. By experimenting with new activities, you're gathering new information, mostly learning about what you *don't* like to do. Sooner or later, you'll uncover a new talent or joy that you possess.

With this joy, you'll have the energy and momentum to be truthful with yourself about the fears that prevent you from getting started in your business. Fear has the power to paralyze us from achieving our desires. By stating your fears out loud, and eventually seeing how they don't make much sense, you take your power back, and gain control over your loftier goals.

Business, in its essence, is nothing more than three systems of operation: creating a product or service, marketing/selling your product or service, and fulfilling the order. Seeing a business in such a basic form can remove the illusion that you can never attain it. Are you recalling those nuggets of valuable business truth? If you're having a rough time believing you can build a business, I urge you to go back and re-read chapters 1-4. Like parenting, new perspectives and concepts take time to absorb. But I guarantee that the lessons I've laid out will always apply to your business, whether at the start or three years in.

The launch of your business is where the journey gets global. Continued exposure for your business is vital for it to thrive. The potential futures and pitfalls were laid out for you in the book so you could anticipate them in your own business. The work on your mission, vision, and values of a business culture gives you more time to focus on your evolution as a business owner.

Protecting what you put so much time and energy into is key to sustaining your business. And finally, I presented and dispelled common misconceptions about the nature of success and what a business involves that could prevent you from taking action.

It takes courage to start a business, as much as it does being a parent. It takes even more courage to do both. I'm well-aware of all the responsibilities you have as a parent. You're the CEO of your household and have obligations to keep the flow of your family's daily routines intact. Deciding to start a business (and learn as you go along), while maintaining the smooth operation of your family, may seem too bold and risky. By committing to this idea, you need to have the faith in yourself that you'll figure out a way to balance both successfully. Such thoughts can be intimidating. Taking action, even in the presence of this fear, is courageous. Committing to yourself, your vision, and your personal growth takes courage. I honor you for your courage in pursuing your business aspirations, even as you juggle your responsibilities and commitments as a parent.

The recurring theme in this book is to figure out what needs to happen for you to take action. *Action* beats any perfect plan that's never acted upon. *Action* is the secret ingredient to success. The difference between someone who is successful and someone who *wishes* they were successful is *action*. All knowledge stems from that one undeniable fact.

I hope this book prompts a shift in your understanding of business. I hope it helps you to see what a business really is, and how you can get started today. I hope it's helped move you from a person *thinking* about taking action to the person who *takes* action.

The hardest part of starting anything new, whether it's creating a business or becoming a first-time parent, is the anticipation time between action and inaction. This anticipation time gives your mind the freedom to imagine scenarios and outcomes of the future that you may experience. Usually those scenarios aren't very positive.

The fear subsides once you're in the "process" of parenting or starting a business because your focus is on the present, on the tasks you need to do right now, *today*. So do you tally up all your parenting wins to see if you qualify to take action toward starting a business? I believe that each of us was born with an innate talent of some kind. Some have the ability to create music; others can develop new products. Trust that the talents and passions that are natural to you are needed to serve the world. The purpose of possessing our gifts is to give them away. Think about your kids, and how you want them to develop in life. If you were to discover in your child a natural talent for, say, singing, wouldn't you want your child to share that gift and continue to sing? How would you feel if your child decided not to sing anymore, in fear of being judged or of experiencing failure? Now how would you feel if your children saw you denying your own talents?

If you have an idea of what people need in their lives, you can turn your vision into reality for others to witness and experience. Automobiles, airplanes, computers, cell phones, and the internet—all were originally thought to be "luxuries," but today, they're "necessities," all pioneered by people with vision. These inventors and visionaries met the entrepreneur's burden of proof: That people needed to have their products in their homes. All these products are now staples in our everyday lives. What we consider everyday life started with someone's vision.

If you have something calling you to take action, and you can't explain what that is or looks like, get curious, and take the steps outlined in this book. If you don't, that itch may never go away, and you'll be left wondering what your life could've been had you only scratched that itch, and took a chance to start a business.

I'm going to reiterate one thing: I don't believe everyone should start a business. Having said that, my message is for you to give yourself the opportunity to discover which side of the equation you belong on, independent of any fear. The only way for you to determine if entrepreneurship is for you is by starting your process and seeing where you land.

If your business idea doesn't work out, and you're still left with the entrepreneurial itch, then you'll know that being a business owner is a path to keep exploring and to start another business. Every successful professional, whether a basketball player, Olympic skier, or a serial entrepreneur, has faced some form of setback or disappointment. What makes them "successful" was the desire to learn from experience, adjust, and keep going.

As a beginning business owner, you have the "game of business" set up for you to win. When you experience the setbacks and "failures" you fear, how you respond will determine whether being an entrepreneur is for you or not.

I concede that the process is indeed scary. As I'm writing this book, I'm starting more businesses and going through this process of fear and joy. I find myself having to listen to my own advice (that's a first) and to get myself to take action along the way. I KNOW the feelings of doubt and inadequacy. I know the fears of failure and rejection. But I also know that the only way this book has validity is by walking the talk.

So, I too join you on this path to finding evermore joy. I dare say that 10, 20, or even 30 years from now, I will be starting more businesses and going through the same steps outlined in this book. I'm sure the process will get easier as I seek to build businesses using talents I didn't even know I possessed. In that sense, creating businesses is my way of discovering more of who I am, and what gifts I have to share. With this discovery comes a fear of the unknown, because I will be embarking on new experiences I've never experienced before. So, while path may not get any easier, it'll be worth the trip.

My trip has led to a very interesting lifestyle that is far simpler than I ever imagined it could be. When I started my business, I believed that all the "bells and whistles" made it a "real" business. I spent years acquiring "stuff," such as a large studio, photo prints for that studio, all the lights, and tools to take photos, hair/makeup, and dressing stations, etc. After a certain point, I realized that none of these things really made me a better business, or a better business owner.

So, I got rid the studio, simplified all my business systems, and reduced the expenses to a fraction of what I used to pay. As a result, I currently work, on average, about 16 hours a month, giving me the freedom to spend more time with my family.

Having all that extra time, I realized how bored I was, not creating or developing something new. That's when I discovered that my joy is in helping others succeed in achieving their own dreams. My joy is seeing other people succeed and knowing I had some part in that success. My passion is seeing you achieve everything you dare to dream.

Having said that, I don't expect you to close this book, and build an empire tomorrow. (If you do, please let me be part of the celebration process!) Many people, myself included, may need extra time and delay the start to their process. You may stall, daydream, and "plan" to take action without ever actually taking action. But before you know it, the benefits of procrastination are no longer valuable. You're tired of staying in that torturous limbo between anticipation and action. You get fed up with the itch, and begin to act.

My process of committing to a new business venture used to start with fear, complaining, whining. Over the years, I trained myself to take that leap of faith, trust in my abilities to "figure it out" as I go, and begin. I'm scared during this process, but I have learned not to let fear delay getting started.

What needs to happen for you to take action? If you DON'T know what business you want to create, here are some action steps you can take:

- Create a list of parenting successes you've experienced and imagine how that success would translate to a business.

- Write down a list of new activities you can try to find joy. Once you have the list, schedule a new activity, once a month.

- Commit to your four hours of exploration per week.

- Brainstorm all the businesses you *could* create, and daydream about how much fun you'd have in running this business.

- Ask other people what they think you'd be good at.

- Look at everything around your house, and realize that everything you possess started with a thought, and a desire to create it. Gather inspiration from your immediate environment that anything is possible.

- Here's a list of action steps if you DO know what business you want to create:

- Write down your ideal vision about what your business looks like when at 100% (storefront, # of clients, your role in the business).

- Write down a day in the life of your business, what you'd be doing and focusing on in your business. Now write down the tasks you don't enjoy in a business (so you know who you'll have to eventually hire).

- Make a list of all the resources you have in making your business a success.

- Enlist (or hire) someone to hold you accountable for taking actions.

- Find a mentor to help guide you through the process of creating your business. If you don't know of anyone, research people who've created businesses similar to what you're after, reach out to them, ask for their advice. You'd be very surprised how many challenges can be solved by just asking for help.

As parents, we constantly learn and adjust to the evolution of our children. When my wife and I had our first son, we tried to keep him on a sleeping schedule. After a few weeks of success, he got sick, and threw the entire schedule off again. With diligent practice, we got him back on a schedule again, only to have that thrown out because of his growth and development. As he got older, we created more routines to help predict the flow of the day, only to be disrupted by social gatherings that throw off the entire routine or having another baby, which threw everything out the window.

This constant cycle of adjustments made something very apparent to me: Parents are resilient. I have the absolute confidence that, with all the qualities you've honed as a parent, you have what it takes to create a successful business. Give yourself the chance to explore. Take a chance on yourself, and create the business you've being itching to create, knowing you have the foundation to succeed. Also, remember that your kids are watching you, every step of the way, learning from you, and your actions. What will they learn when all is said and done?

As Promised

Thank you for taking the time to read my book. I hope that something within these pages inspired you to reflect on your personal situation and consider the idea of starting your own business.

Even though the book has ended, your journey has just begun.

I want to help support you in this endeavor and challenge you to take action on the contents you've learned from this book. So your homework (should you choose to accept it), is to email me at nextsteps@CEOparent.com with the following:

Your ideas of a business you want to get into

Any reasons for not exploring your business further

What you've learned from this book that might help you move forward

A list of 3 action steps you can take immediately to move towards your goal (no matter how big or small the action)

I look forward to hearing from you!

About the Author

Jeremy Cortez is a serial entrepreneur, starting his first business at the age of 19. Even with a BS in Marketing, Jeremy has read hundreds of books and attended countless business seminars all over the US to expand his understanding of entrepreneurialism. With many attempts to create a successful business, it wasn't until after becoming a parent did he experience the entrepreneurial success he desired.

From this success, Jeremy was eager to share his realization of the simplicity of business. Parenting a Business - If You Can Raise a Child, You Can Run a Business is a product of his findings, describing the profound similarities between parenting and running a business. He currently consults with small businesses to Fortune 500 companies on a variety of focuses, from branding to operation systems.

Jeremy resides in San Francisco, CA with his wife and two boys.

www.ingramcontent.com/pod-product-compliance
Lightning Source LLC
Chambersburg PA
CBHW060607200326
41521CB00007B/687